Germany 1918-1933

GERMANY 1918-1933

Revolution, Counter-Revolution and
the Rise of Hitler

Simon Taylor

Duckworth

First published in 1983 by
Gerald Duckworth & Co. Ltd.
The Old Piano Factory
43 Gloucester Crescent, London NW1

ISBN 0 7156 1689 7 (paper)

British Library Cataloguing in Publication Data

Taylor, Simon
  Germany 1918-1933.
  1. Germany—History—1918-1933
  2. Germany—Politics and government—1918-1933
  I. Title
  943.085   DD240

ISBN 0-7156-1689-7

Photoset in North Wales by
Derek Doyle & Associates, Mold, Clwyd
and printed in Great Britain by
The Alden Press, Oxford

Contents

Acknowledgments

I wish to record my thanks to all those who have made this book possible.

The staff of the *Bayerisches Hauptstaatsarchiv*, the *Institut für Zeitgeschichte*, and the *Deutschen Gewerkschaftsbundes* in Munich, the *Archiv Gerstenberg* in Frankfurt, and the *Archiv für Kunst und Geschichte* in Berlin, were generally helpful and patient in coping with my demands upon their time.

Even more important were the efforts of many friends in the Federal Republic who provided me with much information and who were unstinting in their hospitality during numerous visits I made to Germany. I thank especially Erhard Treutner, Heidrun Hoppe, Anna Pietsch, Stefan Rüll, Alexi Hensle, Klaus Feser, Ingrid Hirsmüller, Waggi Herz and Matheus Raab.

But two people in particular have shown me the greatest kindness. To you – Rhiannon and Lydia – I dedicate this book, and hope that in some small way it repays your trust and understanding.

Glossary

Comintern	Communist or Third International
DAP	German Workers Party (precursor of NSDAP)
DNVP	German Nationalist Peoples Party
KPD	German Communist Party
Landbund	Farmers' Association
Landvolk	'Rural People'. Radical protest movement of peasant farmers
Mittelstand	'Middle estate' or middle classes
NSDAP	National Socialist German Workers Party (Nazi)
Reichsbanner	Social Democratic para-military organisation
Reichstag	German National Parliament
Reichswehr	German armed forces
SA	*Sturmabteilung* or Stormtroop, Nazi para-military unit
Spartacists	The *Spartakus* League of revolutionary workers, forerunner of KPD
SPD	German Social Democratic Party
Stahlhelm	'Steel-helmet' – right-wing war veterans' association
SS	*Schutzstaffeln* – elite Nazi bodyguard
USPD	Independent Social Democratic Party
Volk (adjective *völkisch*)	A 'people' or 'race'. The NSDAP called itself a *völkisch* movement
Völkischer Beobachter	National newspaper of NSDAP
Vorwärts	National newspaper of SPD

1

The Workers

I do not believe in the 'evil nature' of man.
I believe that his evil deeds derive from a lack of imagination,
From the indolence of his heart.

(Ernst Toller)

And so on all sides, armament and rearmament; and they will arm to
the point when, one day one side or the other will say; 'Better an end
to this fear than fear without end' ... Then will come the catastrophe!
(August Bebel's Reichstag speech, 9 November 1911)

The prelude to war

On the eve of the First World War the German Social Democratic Party (SPD) was the largest political party in the world. Its one million members and its massive voting strength among the working class made it the largest parliamentary delegation in the German Parliament, or Reichstag. But Germany was not a parliamentary democracy. Although the Reichstag was elected by universal male suffrage, it was powerless to challenge the autocratic regime of the Kaiser. In Prussia, the greatest of the states which made up the German Reich (empire), there was still a three-class voting system, which condemned the Social Democrats to permanent and impotent minority status.

Internationally, however, the SPD was recognised as the guiding light of the Marxist Labour movement. Founded in Gotha in 1875, it was the child of the union of the 'Marxist' Social Democratic Party and the 'Lassallean' (reformist) German Workers' League. Yet despite the revolu-

tionary phraseology of the party leadership and the doctrine of 'class struggle' which forged the consciousness of the rank and file, by the first decade of the twentieth century the SPD was a revolutionary party in name only. Certainly Marx had characterised the seizure of power by the proletariat as a revolution, but his successors among the Social Democratic leadership thought less of the barricades and more and more of a majestic process of historical evolution. Capitalism would go the same way as the dinosaurs, collapsing under the weight of its own contradictions, and the working masses would usher in the golden age of socialism.

The SPD's obligation as the leading member of the Second International was to oppose the outbreak of war with all the means at its disposal, and during the final tense days of July 1914 it organised protest actions and strikes in an effort to disrupt plans for mobilisation. On 1 August, the government declared martial law throughout Germany, making political protest illegal and imposing military censorship. The SPD's attitude to the war was critical.

If they opposed it, the government would use its repressive power to prohibit the party, and even if the political ideals of Social Democracy could survive, the party organisation would be destroyed. Yet the state could scarcely hope to wage a successful war against its external enemies with a major part of the German working class openly hostile.

In the event, however, such arguments were academic, for with a few notable exceptions the SPD leadership ignored their duty to the principles of international socialism and rallied to the defence of their fatherland. What were the reasons for this volte-face? For some it was sheer opportunism – a chance to show the 'nationalist' upper classes that the despised deputies of the working class were also 'good Germans'; co-operation would surely bring political rewards. Others were the victims of clever news manipulation by the German government. The belief that Tsarist Russia – that bastion of autocracy and reaction – was about to fall upon a defenceless Germany encouraged many socialists to call for a 'just' defensive war against 'the threat from the east'. Finally, as even those who maintained their opposition to the war had to admit, the mood among the workers was hardly encouraging. Even if the working class shared little

of the nationalist hysteria displayed by the middle classes, the majority felt a reluctant duty to rally to the aid of their country in the face of apparent external aggression. So, on 4 August 1914, the parliamentary delegation of the SPD, maintaining the tradition of voting en bloc, unanimously supported the government's request for war credits. The previous day, at a closed party caucus, fourteen members had voted for opposition.

'The great patriotic war'

The war brought about a catastrophic collapse of living standards for the German people. Real earnings dropped by 20 to 30 per cent. Average meat consumption fell in 1918 (July) to 12 per cent of its pre-war level, fish consumption to just 5 per cent. Only potatoes were available in anything like their pre-war quantities. Nine million bread-winners were conscripted into the armed forces, while at home disease and starvation took almost as deadly a toll as the battlefield. Shortages of food and fuel were accompanied by inflation. Only those working in the armament industries found

Post-card printed some months before the outbreak of war shows 'the entry of our victorious troops into Paris 1914'.

Einzug unserer siegreichen Truppen in Paris 1914.

2

Edward David justifies the SPD leadership's support for the war at the national Congress of the Social Democratic Party in 1916:

Why did we vote for war credits on August 14th? ... in the east the Czar's army was on the move ... in the west it was the million strong army of the allies, who together with the Russian steamroller, were planning to invade German soil ... An enemy invasion was imminent ... in such a situation it was imperative to do everything that could be done to protect our people.

In reality the 'Kaiser's defensive war' was a pretext for the military ambitions of Germany's aristocratic elite, and the expansionist aims of her industrialists.

The war aims of the German government, from a document written by Reichschancellor Theobald von Bethmann Hollweg, 9 September 1914.

... the general goal of the war ...

The securing of the German Reich's borders to west and east for the conceivable future. In this way, France must be so weakened that she will never rise again to the status of a great power, and Russia must be pushed back as far as possible from Germany's frontiers.

France: a decision from the military point of view as to whether the ceding of Belfort, the western Vosges, the line of fortifications and the coastal strip from Dover to Boulogne is necessary.

In any case, the annexation of the Briey ore-basin, because it is essential for our industry ... a trade agreement which will bring France into economic dependence upon Germany and make it into our export market, thus allowing us to shut out English goods ...

Equally Belgium must, even if it remains a state, sink into vassal status, conceding the right of occupation in a number of militarily important ports, placing its coast at our military disposal, and economically speaking, become a German province ...

Luxemburg will become a German state ...

We will create a central European Economic Union ... which although apparently guaranteeing member countries equal rights, will in fact be under German leadership, and must guarantee German economic rule over central Europe ...

The question of colonial acquisitions, which first and foremost concerns the creation of a centralised Middle African colonial empire ... will be examined later.

Holland ... seemingly independent, but in reality dependent upon us ...

(*Geschichte der deutschen Arbeiterbewegung*, Bd. 2, Berlin 1966)

that wages kept pace with the increasing cost of living; and here, as elsewhere, the government arbitrarily suspended protective labour legislation and increased the working day to twelve or thirteen hours. Yet, while the masses toiled and starved, and the front claimed six million victims, an indifferent administration made paltry efforts to halt a flourishing black market which allowed the wealthy to live in comfort and the owners of industry to make fortunes out of the supply of armaments and munitions. The result was strikes and food riots, especially in the large towns and cities.

Under normal conditions this discontent would have been organised and channelled by the unions. But the union leadership was co-operating with the military regime to further the war effort, and with the authorities ever ready to conscript militant workers into the army, factory-based opposition was forced underground and gradually came into contact with political radicals opposed to the war. Of these radical groups the Spartacists and the Independent Social Democrats (who split from the Majority Social Democrats during the course of the war) were the most important. They were to play the predominant role in the unfolding of the

German Revolution. None the less, their organisational basis among the German workers was weak, and their ranks were so frequently reduced by imprisonment and repression that actions could only be loosely co-ordinated among the centres of radical discontent – Berlin, Brunswick, Stuttgart and Bremen.

The great impetus to revolt was provided by events in Russia which began to unfold in March 1917. The onward march of the Russian revolutionaries inspired all those who believed that a rapid end to the war and a just peace in Germany could come about through the political action of the masses. Yet the experience of the Russian Revolution served to highlight the differences of strategy among radical groups in Germany to the task of over-throwing the autocratic military regime. The SPD (or the Majority Social Democrats as they were now called) were still firmly wedded to their policy of supporting the war-effort and the government, despite rumblings of discontent among significant sections of the party as the expansionist character of the war became increasingly apparent. The Independent Social Democrats (USPD), who broke away from the mother party in April 1917, were an uneasy coalition of centrists and radicals whose

---

By the end of the First World War, nearly twice as many women were employed in the factories as in 1913. The radical Karl Retzlaw remembers conditions in the factory at the end of 1917:

… They told me their stories of husbands and fathers at the front; of their children looked after by grandparents and neighbours, or shut up inside the house. Even from the unmarried girls there was only one question, 'when will the war end?'. Here I could come out openly against the war, and I was listened to with great interest … The working conditions were like they must have been during the first industrial revolution. There was always 'something wrong', especially during the night-shift. Never a night passed without one or more of the women collapsing at their machines because of exhaustion, hunger or illness.

(Karl Retzlaw, *Spartacus. Aufstieg und Niedergang. Erinnerungen eines Parteiarbeiters*, Frankfurt 1967)

Karl Liebknecht

'Whether in France or in Germany it is the same clique who mint gold from the discord among people ... You shout, 'The fatherland is in danger!' yet it is not in danger from an external enemy, but from the most dangerous of internal enemies – namely the international armaments industry' (Liebknecht in the Reichstag, April 1913)

Liebknecht was the sole member of the Reichstag to vote against war-credits in 1914. On 12 January 1916 he was expelled from the SPD's Reichstag faction, and later in the year he was sentenced to four-and-a-half years hard labour for his outspoken opposition to the war. On 15 January 1919 he was murdered by army officers.

opposition to the war was their only real point of agreement. In fact the left wing of the USPD shared many of the revolutionary tendencies of the Spartacists, grouped around Karl Liebknecht and Rosa Luxemburg, even if they did not share the latter's belief in the 'revolutionary will of the proletariat' and an insistence upon agitation at the expense of organisation.

The first significant sign of revolt came in 1917 when the German authorities uncovered a widespread anti-war movement among the sailors and stokers of the North Sea fleet which was threatening to erupt into open mutiny. Although it was repressed, the naval command could not destroy the opposition, which took on an openly radical character and in time lit the fuse of the German revolution. Indeed, when the Kaiser and his military dictators failed to honour a pledge to carry through even limited democratic reforms, the Majority Social Democratic leadership made it clear that their patience was wearing thin. In January 1918 a strike of munitions workers, which threatened to cripple armaments manufacture, was headed off only with the greatest difficulty, and the Social Democrats warned that, unless concessions were made to the war-weary masses, they would be forced to withdraw their support from the government. Then, suddenly, early in 1918, the military situation eased and the supply of food for the home population improved. For a time it seemed that the socialist leaders' patriotism would have its reward in a German military victory.

The sudden improvement in Germany's fortunes was a result of the annexationist peace agreement which was forced upon the new Bolshevik regime in Russia in March 1918. Now able to concentrate military resources on the western front, the military leadership opened a major offensive early in the summer. But after initial successes the offensive came to a halt, and by August the German armies were in retreat. The military machine had shot its bolt. An allied breakthrough was imminent, and in September the military dictator General Ludendorff admitted to the government that only an immediate cease-fire could prevent a military catastrophe on Germany's borders. For the political rulers and the economic masters of Germany the task of the moment was to 'save what can be saved'. Or, as the industrialist Robert Bosch explained to the pro-

5

The defeated German army streams back across the Rhein at Mannheim.

crastinating Secretary of State: 'when the house is burning you may have to put out the fire with water from a cesspool, even if it stinks a bit afterwards' (letter to Haussman, 24 October 1918). The 'stink' was democracy, and in order to secure a favourable peace settlement with the allies and smother the revolution which threatened at home, the Majority Socialists were brought into the government, precisely to 'put out the fire'.

From the outset the Majority Socialists operated from a position of extreme weakness. The old oligarchy wanted to use them as a tool – to call the masses to order and to prevent the revolution from below by carrying out a 'revolution from above'. But the masses were in political ferment, and radical demands to sweep away all vestiges of the imperial state were finding an echo, not only among the workers, but even among sections of the middle classes. The Majority Socialists denounced the Spartacists and radicals as 'agents of Bolshevik chaos', yet the imperial establishment, and in particular the armed forces, refused the SPD leaders' demands for the abdication of the Kaiser and an end to the suppression of political rights.

The impotence of the new 'liberal' government and the token nature of the Majority Socialists' position within it were dramatically demonstrated at the end of October, when the German navy under Admiral Scheer put to sea for a final battle with the overwhelmingly superior British North Sea Fleet. The government knew nothing of this plan, which was intended to satisfy the 'honour' of the military hierarchy at the cost of several thousand lives, when Germany was already suing for peace. But sailors at Wilhelmshaven refused to provision the ships or put to sea. The mutiny spread through the fleet to the dock-workers of Kiel. Suddenly posters appeared demanding not just peace but 'the destruction of militarism, the ending of social injustice and the overthrow of the ruling class' (from a report by Kiel police officer Hager, 2 November 1918). The German revolution had begun!

Sailors at Wilhelmshaven refuse orders to put to sea for a final naval battle against the British fleet.

The November Revolution

During the first week of November a revolutionary wave spread from the North Sea coast to the main cities and industrial areas of Germany as councils of workers and soldiers seized power from the imperial authorities. On 9 November the revolution reached Berlin. Radical groups in Berlin – especially the Revolutionary Shop Stewards' Committees (based in the large factories), the Spartacists and the Independent Socialists – had been organising for an uprising on 4 November. In the event they postponed their action, unaware of the mutiny in the fleet. Now they found themselves overtaken by the swiftness of the mass movement.

The 'liberal' cabinet met in emergency session on 7 November, with the SPD leaders thoroughly alarmed at a state of affairs which they felt they could barely control. As Philip Scheidemann bluntly stated, 'we have done all we can to keep the masses on the halter'. Unless reforms were forthcoming – most obviously the abdication of the Kaiser – the SPD would resign (minutes of war-cabinet, 7 November 1918). Unsure of success in this direction, the SPD leadership also met regularly with worker representatives, hoping to make a bid for political leader-

Clara Zetkin addresses an assembly of the Social Democratic Party. A left-wing critic of the SPD leadership, she said of them:

'What they want, it sounds laughable I know, is revolution without revolution ... the revolutionary vocabulary of Marxism is maintained with religious fervour, but its meaning has evaporated.'

ship if an insurrection should break out.

Late in the evening of 8 November the call went out from the Berlin Revolutionary Committee for a General Strike. Next day, as tens of thousands of workers, some armed, took to the streets, to be joined by sections of the Berlin garrison and naval detachments from the North Sea fleet, the SPD threw in its lot with the revolutionaries. By midday the Kaiser had announced his abdication and the cabinet of Prince Max Baden had resigned. The SPD leader, Friedrich Ebert, was appointed Chancellor. His first act was to appeal to the masses to leave the streets; the major priority of a socialist government was, he stated, 'the maintenance of law and order' (*Vorwärts*, 9 November 1918, special edition).

The SPD moved quickly to consolidate its tenuous foothold, particularly among the soldiers, for whom the new nationalist credentials of the Majority Socialists were more acceptable than the internationalist beliefs of working-class radicals. The election of deputies for the Soldiers' Councils resulted in a majority declaring support for the SPD, though many took at face value the SPD leadership's promise to be a 'revolutionary government' which would 'carry out a socialist programme'. Even so, the Independents and radicals were well organised among the factory workers, and for a time it seemed likely that the radical-led Factory Councils would provide a left-wing opposition to the SPD with their power base in the Soldiers' Councils. At the last moment, however, SPD appeals for working-class unity caught the mood of the masses, and the principle of 'parity of representation' was implemented. So, despite elections which had given radical leaders a clear mandate in the Factory Councils, equal numbers of Majority and Independent Socialists were appointed as factory representatives as an expression of the 'united revolutionary will of the proletariat'. In reality, as Richard Müller, the leader of the Berlin Shop Stewards, acidly noted, the Factory

Councils thereby lost their independent and revolutionary character. 'Social Democrats were elected as members of the Workers' Councils who the day before had been driven out of the factories with blows because they would not join the General Strike.'

It seemed that the November Revolution had passed off with very little bloodshed. The workers returned to the factories on 12 November, expecting the new National Executive Council (made up of three Independent and three Majority Socialists) to put into practice the oft-repeated promise to build a democratic socialist society from the ruins of the old order. The Social Democratic Party press proudly trumpeted their achievements:

> The revolution has been brilliantly carried through ... the solidarity of proletarian action has smashed all opposition. Total victory all along the line. A victory made possible because of the unity and determination of all who wear the workers' shirt ('Unity is a Duty'. From an article in *Norddeutsches Volksblatt* (MSPD) 15 November 1918).

In fact, as Rosa Luxemburg wrote, the November events were a Pyrrhic victory for the workers. While the armistice, the abolition of the autocratic monarchy and the introduction of universal suffrage were fruits of the revolution, the real power of the old regime was still entrenched in the twin strongholds of the military and heavy industry. And in turn the two issues which divided the reformist right-wing of the SPD from the Independents and the Spartacists concerned the creation of a workers' militia and the socialisation of key industries.

It was apparent from the outset that Ebert and his SPD colleagues intended to equivocate indefinitely over the issue of nationalising German heavy industry. Ebert in particular feared to take any action which might disrupt supplies of food or fuel at a time of general shortages, while the Minister for the Economy, Dr August Müller, announced that, 'the world is not

Food riots, which at first were spontaneous outbursts of popular unrest,
frequently developed into political demonstrations against the war and
the military dictatorship. *Above* In Hamburg the owners of a potted meat
factory where 'vile goings on have been reported' are led through the
streets by an infuriated crowd (the nature of these 'vile goings on' can only
be guessed at!). *Below* In Halle a department store is plundered and set
on fire. Some elements used the political unrest as a cover for criminal
activities, allowing the government to represent radical elements as
'thieves and plunderers'.

Ebert (far left) and Scheidemann (far right) greet
German troops returning from the front.

yet ready for general socialisation, so we
may not permit ourselves any experimen-
tation in this area' (*Deutsche Allgemeine
Zeitung*, 29 December 1918). But the
threat of counter-revolution was much
more immediate. Indeed the radical left
consistently warned that the imperial
military hierarchy was still intact despite
the events of November, for during
December the old guard, under army
generals Groener and Lequis, twice
attempted military coups, only to be foiled
by alert revolutionary soldiers, deserting
troops or their own incompetence. But
what was most worrying for the workers
organised in the Factory Councils, as well
as for the Independents on the Executive
Council was the apparent ambivalence (if
not the actual connivance) of Ebert and his
colleague Scheidemann in the attempted
coups.

In fact there is ample evidence to link
Ebert to General Groener's plan to 'clean
up the capital' with troops loyal to the
Kaiser as early as 10 November. Certainly
a secret telephone link did exist between

the two men, which no other member of the
Executive Council knew about. Groener
later testified that his aim in reaching
accommodation with Ebert was to 'win a
share of power in the new state for the
army and the officer corps ... to preserve
the best and strongest elements of old
Prussia' (Groener's testimony to a Munich
court in the 'Dolchstossprozess', 1925).
Ebert's motives were more complex.
Certainly his fear of 'Bolshevism' overcame
any reluctance he may have felt to use the
forces of reaction to crush a radical
insurrection. But, whether through naivety
or (as some claimed) treachery, he never
shrank from using the armed power of the
far-right to impose the government's will
upon recalcitrant workers, irrespective of
the long-term effects of such a policy on the
stability of parliamentary democracy.
Thus attempts to found a loyal, democratic
workers' militia were abandoned almost at
the outset, for fear that such a force would
be tainted with radicalism. Instead the
Majority Social Democrats put their trust
in the Freecorps – heavily armed 'reliable'
mercenary units, invariably under the
command of right-wing officers. These
'defenders of democracy' were viciously

anti-socialist military freebooters, and in later years Freecorps volunteers were to provide many of the leaders of the Nazi party.

The strain between the Independents and the Majority Socialists in the Executive Council reached breaking point on Christmas eve. The People's Naval Division, which consistently supported the radicals, had been a thorn in Ebert's side as he tried to 'impose order' in Berlin. After a confrontation over the government's failure to pay the sailors, the Naval Division surrounded the Chancellery and arrested Otto Wels, one of the SPD Executive members. Seizing their chance Groener and Lequis demanded excitedly that their troops be sent into action against the 'rebels'; but Ebert refused, asserting that a settlement could be reached by negotiation. In response Groener threatened to withdraw the army's backing for the SPD leadership. Not long after a rumour was heard that Wels's life was in danger. Ebert capitulated and ordered the attack. However, a sharp artillery bombardment failed to dislodge the Naval

Men of the People's Naval Division in the Marstall building in Berlin.

Division (thereby genuinely putting Wels's life in danger), and when armed workers arrived on the scene Groener's army unit withdrew.

The Independent Socialists on the Executive had not been informed of Ebert's decision to attack, despite the real danger that such action could have provoked a bloodbath. At a crisis meeting of the Executive, Ebert and his SPD colleagues suppressed all mention of Groener's ultimatum. Unable to force the resignation of the SPD faction, the Independents had no choice but to resign from the government themselves. The departure of the Independents marked the last act of the German Revolution, but it proved to be the first step on the path towards civil war.

The Independents were themselves divided, however, particularly on the attitude to be adopted to the proposed National Assembly, which was to take over as the supreme legislature of the new republic (the National Assembly was the corner-stone of the Majority Socialists' programme for democratic reform, and a National Congress of Soldiers and Workers Councils endorsed the decision to hold nationwide elections in the first quarter of 1919). Although many Independents were

The Executive Committee of Independents and Majority Social Democrats. Left to right Barth, Landesberg, Ebert, Haase, Dittmann, Scheidemann

Minutes of cabinet meetings of the Executive Council

13 December 1918 [on the army and the Soldiers' Councils]

Landesberg [Majority Social Democrat]: In the case of the officers all the trouble was caused by a few fools, whereas the institution of the Workers' and Soldiers' Councils amounts to the organisation of chaos.

28 December 1918 [The Social Democrats discuss matters of state]

[In a long and heated debate over who was responsible for giving the order for the troops to attack the sailors of the Peoples' Naval Division, it was established that the sailors were originally demanding their back-pay before giving up the keys to the castle where they had been billeted. A soldier's deputy had taken the keys to Barth, who had then telephoned Wels to authorise payment to the sailors. When the sailors went to Wels however, he refused to pay, saying that he did not have the keys himself. During the discussion the following exchange is recorded]

Barth: ... When I awoke on the 24th, ... my wife came in and told me, 'They are firing artillery in Berlin.' 'Good grief no' I said, 'surely it is the dustcarts being unloaded.' At that moment my driver appeared.
Landesberg: So you have a chauffeur! I don't!
Barth: I have to get right across Berlin every day ...
Dittmann: Scheidemann comes in by car every day from Steglitz too. I walk.
Landesberg: Well it looks like we are the only proletarians.

26 December 1918 [attitudes to political dissent]

Scheidemann: In the *Red Flag* [the newspaper of the radicals] you will find Ebert, Landesberg and myself — myself most of all — called 'murderers, bloodhounds and scoundrels' every day. You will read 'Down with this disgraceful government'. *Freiheit* [paper of the Independents] avoids the term 'bloodhounds' but it shreds us to pieces anyway. So you can imagine the mood that is being created in working-class circles susceptible to such ideas ... in short we must decide where we stand on the question of deserters who demand 40,000 marks at gunpoint ... these men who invaded *Vorwärts* (the Social Democratic newspaper offices) are a completely unscrupulous gang ...
Dittmann: ... Of course there are a few officers who are capable of the most absurd plots, but they don't amount to anything. On the other hand there are those who want to smash everything, and who put the revolution in danger ...

12

Above Wels addresses a sitting of the Soldiers' Council in the Reichstag building, Berlin. Soldiers had little contact with the pre-war and wartime revolutionary movement. Otto Wels, a member of the Majority SPD executive committee, moved in quickly after 9 November to exert influence upon the Berlin garrison. As a result, the elections for the Soldier's Councils provided a clear majority for the SPD – an important influence on future events.

Below Däumig warns the First Congress of Workers' and Soldiers' Councils (December 1918) against voting for an immediate convening of the National Assembly.

... When the history of these revolutionary weeks in Germany is written, people will smile and say: 'Were they blind? Couldn't they see that they were putting a rope round their own necks?' For any clear thinking person must see that the jubilant approval of the National Assembly is equivalent to passing the death sentence on the council system ... And if you are bent upon forming a club for political suicides, go ahead! I, for one, refuse to take part.

[The council system] is and must be the natural form of organisation in a modern revolution. Certainly I accept – and here I address my remarks chiefly to our comrades in uniform – that the system is tainted with the nasty smell of bolshevism ... Well comrades ... what is not called bolshevism nowadays? All of you here today, are in the eyes of many people, bolsheviks.

... On 6 November, when we had distributed our last leaflets, a proclamation of the Social Democratic Party had this to say: 'Beware of a split, of fraternal war among the workers and of the incitement of irresponsible elements who wish to entice you ... '. But when 9 November came; when by virtue of our organisation in the factories and the barracks, the old system was swept away, they came down here in droves in order to take part in that very same council system!

... Comrade Cohen and others have asserted that the council system will continue to exist if a National Assembly comes into being: that is nothing but noise and hot air. What is a council system to do alongside a parliamentary bourgeois democratic system ... (it will be) a mere figure in a landscape, a marionette! In the economic sphere the old-style trade unions, aided by the National Assembly, and the middle classes will push the workers' councils out of the factories. They have already done so, and are doing so.

The systems are irreconcilable – we must choose one or the other. But I tell you now; under the old-style system you will not attain your dream of a new, culturally and intellectually free Germany – a Germany free of that old spirit of submission which is even today deeply rooted in the German people ...

13

uneasy about participating in an election before a fundamental attempt to neutralise the old army and purge the administration of anti-democratic tendencies, they accepted the need for a rapid changeover to parliamentary government. At this point the Spartacists broke away from the USPD, arguing that the time had come to found a genuinely revolutionary German workers' party based on the power of the Factory Councils. On 30 December, the Spartacists and other radical groups met to found what was to become the German Communist Party (KPD). Rosa Luxemburg and Karl Liebknecht, the spiritual mentors of the wartime revolutionary movement, were accepted as the founding figures of the new party. But in the acrimonious atmosphere of a sectarian struggle between 'reformist' and 'revolutionary' tendencies, Rosa Luxemburg's appeal for the delegates to endorse a policy of 'educating the working class' was ignored. Despite her plea that crude 'either-or' choices were a gross over-simplification of the political situation, and that the task of the new party was to enter the elections in an attempt to 'enlighten and educate the mass of the people', it was policies and slogans promising immediate 'revolutionary' results that won the day. Thus began the career of the German Communist Party – from the outset it was a bitter disappointment for Rosa Luxemburg, the most original thinker of the German left, whose personal destiny was to mirror so tragically the fate of the party which she led.

The 'January events'

The first main clash between the Majority Socialists and groups of radical workers occurred in January 1919, when the SPD-dominated Prussian government tried to dismiss the popular Emil Eichhorn from his post as police chief of Berlin. The USPD and the shop stewards committee called for a mass protest against this act, which could only be considered inflam-

Rosa Luxemburg

'The masses must be made aware of the fact that they can determine their own destiny' (19 May 1914).

matory, given the tense political atmosphere in the capital. The response was a demonstration in the streets of Berlin which was so overwhelming that a number of revolutionary groups occupied the city's main newspaper buildings in the belief that the time was ripe to carry forward the revolution. Radical leaders suddenly found themselves in a dangerous predicament. Unable to persuade the workers to evacuate the buildings, which included the offices of the Social Democratic newspaper *Vorwärts*, they nevertheless held the government responsible for the affair, because of its provocation. At first the

A massive demonstration led by radicals and Independent Socialists winds its way down the Siegesallee on 7 January 1919. As the head of the procession reached the Tiergarten, central Berlin's largest park, a steward addressed the demonstration through a loud-hailer: 'Comrades, maintain revolutionary discipline. Do not walk on the grass!'

Majority Socialist leaders showed themselves willing to hold talks, unsure of their ability to flush out the insurgents by force. But a large Freecorps was being assembled outside Berlin, and after two days of negotiations the cabinet began to feel confident that they could destroy the radical threat once and for all. Having unsuccessfully demanded the evacuation of the *Vorwärts* building as a precondition for further talks, the Freecorps were ordered to storm the premises. Bloody street fighting broke out and continued for several days, interrupted only by a huge workers' demonstration which demanded an end to the violence in the name of socialist unity. The leadership of the USPD and the KPD acted swiftly by expelling members who had taken part in the occupation, but the damage had been done, and the entire Berlin workers' movement was to pay the price.

The government seized the opportunity to 'pacify' the city before the elections scheduled for 19 January, and the First Freecorps was allowed formally to occupy the city. But the brutality of the troops far exceeded any policy of pacification. Suspects were arrested in the streets and arbitrarily executed. Known radicals were 'shot while resisting arrest'. Others simply disappeared after being taken into custody; when their bodies were discovered in the capital's canals they were said to have escaped and drowned. After Rosa Luxemburg and Karl Liebknecht

Above Armed Spartacists march through Berlin shortly before the occupation of the newspaper buildings.

Below Street-fighting in the newspaper quarter. Radicals defend their positions, using rolls of newsprint as barricades.

The *Vorwärts* building after bombardment by heavy
artillery and storming by the Freecorps.

Above Government troops in front of Berlin Castle.

Below A dead 'Spartacist' is collected from the street and carried away.

were abducted and murdered by Free-corps officers, even the Majority Socialists protested – but they were powerless to restrain the terror they had unleashed. The 'January events', as they became known, left a legacy of deep bitterness among the Berlin workers. And as the scenario was repeated throughout the cities and industrial towns of Germany, the Social Democratic Minister in charge of the armed forces, Gustav Noske, earned himself the name of the 'Bloodhound'.

Outside Berlin the most serious challenge to the elections for a National Assembly came from Bremen. On 10 January Communists and radicals proclaimed the city a Workers' Republic under the leadership of the local Soldiers' and Workers' Councils (the German word is *Räterepublik*, which means a 'council-republic'; it is analagous to the concept of a republic of self-governing soviets on the early Russian model). But the radicals again misjudged the political mood of the

---

Cabinet minutes, 15 January 1919, on the 'excesses' of the government troops.

Ebert: ... The Independent's party headquarters was not sacked by Noske's troops, but probably at the instigation of the Reichstag commandant. The culprits will be severely dealt with. We have consistently warned the troops to proceed with caution, but in view of the large numbers involved such wrongs cannot be completely avoided ... In Trebbin the soldiers also proceeded ruthlessly. An investigation was immediately undertaken and the culprits will be charged with their crimes.

(No soldier was ever charged with any crime carried out in 'pursuit of duty'.) *Untrue* *Pbs 2*

Cabinet minutes, 21 January 1919, Noske on the use of force.

Noske: ... The government must be able to back up its authority with might. We have raised 22,000 men in a military unit during the course of the week. In two or three weeks we will be in a position to restore a certain amount of order; dealings with the Soldiers' Councils have therefore taken on a different character. Hitherto the Soldiers' Councils have had force on their side; now this is in our favour. For Berlin we require 10,000 men ... Maercker's corps will protect Weimar, and it will re-establish order in Halle and Braunschweig in passing. We will restore order in Bremen in the course of this week, and then only Cuxhaven will be left, because we are prevented from attacking via Altonia. We might restore order there via Schleswig, and if necessary the resistence in Hamburg will be put down by force ...

---

workers, and subsequently had to agree to hold elections for the National Assembly. Even so, given the bloody events in Berlin, the workers' leaders were unwilling to concede their local authority to the central government. Once more the Executive Council in Berlin refused all attempts at conciliation, and Noske ordered the Gerstenberg Freecorps to march into Bremen on the patently false pretext that food supplies from the port were being blockaded. While the majority of the Bremen workers had been lukewarm in their support of the Communists, and indeed the Soldiers' and Workers' Councils had themselves overturned the decision to boycott the National elections, they had no intention either of allowing the city to be occupied by reactionary mercenaries. The result was resistance, street battles and bloody reprisals.

'Socialisation is on the march'

The fall of Bremen marked the end of the first phase of the civil war – a phase marked by ill-judged radical putsches and the vicious reaction of the Freecorps. After the elections for the National Assembly on 19 January, a second phase opened, substantially different in character from the first. This involved attempts by organised groups of workers, in particular the coal-miners of the Ruhr basin, to improve their living standards through campaigns of political and industrial protest. In the main they were demanding that the government honour pledges to nationalise

19

Miners arrive at the pithead – underground shifts averaged ten hours.

the coal-mines and other key industries.

Wildcat strikes erupted in the mines early in 1919 as a protest against delays in carrying through socialisation proposals. At first the government seemed to work towards an accommodation with the miners' demands that a Factory Council system of management be introduced into the industry. Unfortunately the two sides held widely different views on the powers to be assigned to the Councils, and on 6 February the miners issued an ultimatum calling for a General Strike if the government refused to concede the principle of workers' co-determination. As the strike deadline approached, a hasty compromise was agreed, though this collapsed when the army marched into the radical stronghold of Hervest-Dorsten. Even so, the government's tactics disrupted the strike movement sufficiently to prevent any effective co-ordination between the various groups of workers, and for a time it seemed as if the unrest would peter out. Once again, however, the aggressive tactics of the occupying military forces soon stoked

up a powerful head of resentment and anger.

In April a new strike broke out – this time crippling coal production for three weeks. The miners demanded shorter working hours, wage increases and, most significantly, the disarming of the Freecorps in the Ruhr. The new government (a coalition of Majority Socialists and members of the Democratic and Centre Parties which came to power after the National Assembly elections) reacted by declaring martial law. The inevitable result was confrontation and bloodshed, and only the intervention of the respected union leader Carl Severing prevented a serious escalation of the dispute. His compromise formula, forced on the exhausted miners, was sufficient to establish an uneasy peace in the mining industry for the remainder of 1919.

The government's aggressive response to the strikes in the Ruhr and to a General Strike in Halle (which until the intervention of troops had been quite without violence) generated immense disquiet in Berlin. Even workers' leaders normally loyal to the SPD resented the bloody repression carried out in the name of Social Democracy, and when elections for the Factory Councils swept away the old SPD majority in the capital a new mood of revolutionary fervour became apparent. The government was so clearly alarmed at the situation that the SPD minister, Philip Scheidemann, having announced the government's categorical refusal to incorporate Factory Councils into the proposed constitution, announced a week later that this was a 'misunderstanding' and that the council system would be included. On 2 March it was officially announced, 'Socialisation is on the march'! Forty-eight hours later, when a General Strike seemed imminent, placards appeared announcing 'Socialisation has arrived'!

Taking government declarations at their face value, the Majority Socialists and unions in Berlin withdrew their call for

1. The Workers

Freecorps heavy mortars in place in Alexanderplatz, Berlin.

mass action and dissolved the General Strike co-ordinating committee. Incensed workers, against the orders of their leaders, tried to take matters into their own hands and shut off the city's water, gas and electricity supplies. Looting broke out, and later a police station was attacked. Now the strike could be portrayed as open rebellion, and Noske, on the pretext that Spartacists had murdered sixty captured police officers, sent in the Freecorps. Fearing wide-scale violence and inevitable killings, the strike leaders called off their action on 8 March. It was too late. Street battles had already erupted in the eastern suburbs, where aircraft and heavy artillery were used against the workers. Martial law was proclaimed, and any proletarian suspected of carrying arms risked instant execution. The street battles became a massacre, as over 1200 workers lost their lives – many executed in reprisal for the murder of the Berlin police officers. When the fighting finally died down, all but two of the 'murdered' policemen were found to be alive. One had been killed in the street fighting; the fate of the other was never determined. It was nine months before the state of seige was lifted in Berlin, a period in which unemployment rose dramatically and shortages of food and housing became acute. For the workers it seemed that even the meagre benefits of the revolution were being whittled away.

By the end of 1919 the Factory Council Bill was the issue of the moment. The bill put before the Reichstag demolished any lingering hopes that the workers' councils could provide a basis for the democratisation of industry, even on a local scale. Only a pale shadow of the much promised policy of workers' co-determination in economic matters remained, and it was widely believed that the reorganised Factory Councils would be simply a rubber stamp for management decisions. On this issue the Independent Social Democrats determined to make a stand, sure of their support among the

21

'Shot after summary court-martial.'

A rating from the People's Naval Division describes his imprisonment and capture during the March fighting:

Suddenly a voice shouted 'Hands up!'. For a moment I thought it was a joke and I called out 'Stop acting the fool'. It was not a joke … I was taken to a cellar where I found over a hundred other prisoners … in the end there were about three hundred of us in there … At midday, the commandant, Lieutenant Marloh arrived. The prisoners were paraded in front of him. To each he gave an order, 'To the left, to the right.' I had to go to the left … we did not know what was going to happen to us. Suddenly we heard shots, and thought our people had come to the rescue. But it was something else … Eventually we were taken out into the street. As we passed through the courtyard the order was given to turn our heads to the left. I risked a glance to the right. Our comrades lay in a heap against a blood-spattered wall.

(Ernst Brossat, *Mit der Volksmarinedivision im Kampf gegen die Konterrevolution*, p. 329, in *Weimarer Republik*, Köln 1977, p. 158).

Mass demonstration in front of the Reichstag on 13 January 1920, immediately before army units opened fire killing 41 and wounding over 100.

Berlin workers. They even took the precaution of expelling Communists from the Council leadership, fearful of another putschist debacle. In the Ruhr, and in Germany's other principal coalmining region of Upper Silesia, the deep disquiet over the government's plans looked certain to provoke a further crisis, while on the railways strike action also loomed.

On 13 January tens of thousands of Berlin workers and their families staged a protest outside the Reichstag building as delegates met to put the finishing touches to the Factory Council Bill. The meeting was peaceful, but after the speeches the crowds milled around, reluctant to disperse. Then shots rang out, and troops under the command of General Lüttwitz opened fire on the demonstrators with machine guns. Within seconds 42 lay dead and 105 wounded. Claiming that the demonstration was an insurrection, Noske again declared a state of seige throughout northern Germany and ordered the suppression of the USPD. But, as government documents later made clear, it was the threat of strikes and the need to obtain

Noske (right) in consultation with General Lüttwitz.

'I guarantee that no unnecessary blood will flow. I will clean up – not exterminate. I will bring peace and freedom with the new republican army ...'
(Noske in *Vorwärts*, 12 January 1919).

23

SEIGE

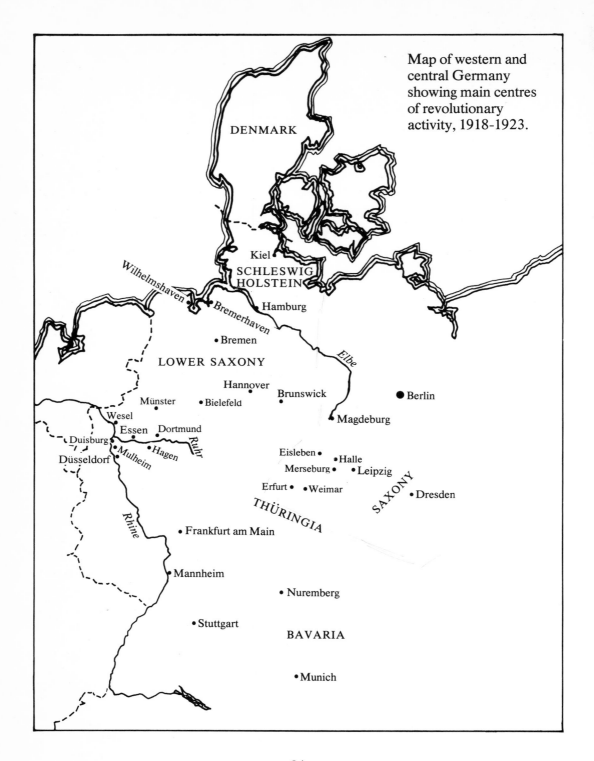

Map of western and
central Germany
showing main centres
of revolutionary
activity, 1918-1923.

DENMARK

Kiel

SCHLESWIG
HOLSTEIN

Wilhelmshaven

Bremerhaven

Hamburg

Bremen

Elbe

LOWER SAXONY

Hannover

Brunswick

Berlin

Münster

Bielefeld

Magdeburg

Wesel

Essen

Dortmund

Duisburg

Ruhr

Hagen

Mulheim

Eisleben

Halle

Düsseldorf

Merseburg

Leipzig

Erfurt

Weimar

SAXONY

Dresden

Rhine

THÜRINGIA

Frankfurt am Main

Mannheim

Nuremberg

Stuttgart

BAVARIA

Munich

Captain Ehrhardt (centre in overcoat) in the government quarter of Berlin.

marched through the Brandenberg Gate and occupied the government quarter. Lüttwitz's political convictions were concise if simple-minded:

> We need two things. Order and work ... Only compulsion makes people work. He who doesn't work, won't eat! Secondly a complete ban on strikes ... agitators will be exterminated without compassion (letter to Noske, 1 September 1919).

The reaction of the workers in Berlin and throughout Germany was immediate and united – a General Strike which crippled all attempts by Lüttwitz and the provisional junta leader Kapp to govern.

The military authorities in northern and eastern Germany declared openly for the counter-revolutionaries, and clashes between hostile crowds and the army were reported in Frankfurt, Leipzig and Kiel. On 15 March 59 workers were killed when troops opened fire in Dresden. The proletariat armed and organised, and pitched battles between workers' militias and army units spread across the country. Around Halle a battle raged for three days, ending only when the military forces withdrew from the city. But it was the Ruhr which once again experienced the most bitter fighting. Here army units enthusiastically supported the putsch in Berlin, and General von Watter sent his troops into the mining towns to crush any resistance.

This time, however, the soldiers met fiercely determined and well-armed miners, who surrounded the first Freecorps detachment and after a lengthy battle forced its surrender. Next day, 16 March, a larger detachment was driven out of the area after heavy losses. The three working-class parties, the KPD, the USPD and the SPD, set about organising a Red Army of the Ruhr, with a centralised leadership and a chain of command based in Hagen. At the height of the conflict nearly a hundred thousand workers were involved in the struggle with the counter-revolutionary forces. On 18 March the whole of the Westphalian sector of the Ruhr had been

special powers to deal with political unrest outside Berlin which were the real *raison d'être* for Noske's proclamation of martial law.

The Kapp putsch

Within a month, however, Noske had more pressing problems to deal with. At the end of February he ordered the 'Ehrhardt Brigade' – one of the most hated and feared of the Freecorps units – to disband. General Lüttwitz refused, and in turn issued an ultimatum for the dissolution of the National Assembly. When Ebert and Noske ignored the ultimatum General Lüttwitz ordered Ehrhardt and his men to march on Berlin. At six o'clock in the morning the Social Democratic ministers fled the capital, and a few minutes later Freecorps soldiers

Above Soldiers taking part in the Kapp putsch in Berlin display propaganda posters assuring the populace that it is not a pro-monarchist coup.

Left An overfull commuter train manned by military personnel attempts to break the General Strike.

Below Soldiers break up a meeting of striking metal workers in Berlin.

26

Kapp – the man who gave his name to the putsch – fled to Sweden when the coup failed.

march north and reoccupy the district (the *Reichswehr* was the term given to the limited German army permitted under the peace treaty with the allies). Clearly the workers' stronghold was strategically isolated; negotiations were the only realistic course of action.

The leadership's united front held firm, and negotiators agreed to demobilise the Red Army if guarantees were forthcoming about creating a new democratic army to replace the hated Freecorps. An agreement was signed, known as the Bielefeld Treaty, promising the democratisation of the German army and the creation of local workers' militias in the Ruhr. In return the Red Army would be stood down, provided the Reichswehr was kept out of the area in future, as the government promised. It seemed at first that a bloodless solution had been found. Unfortunately the legal complexities of the situation were lost upon many of the workers, who felt that their sacrifices had been in vain, and that the government would renege on this agreement just as they had reneged upon their promises of nationalisation. Convinced of imminent betrayal, a radical core of Red Army soldiers re-grouped in Mülheim under the leadership of syndicalists and dissident Communists. The political unity and the will of the workers disintegrated, and when the Reichswehr was ordered back into the Ruhr it met only isolated pockets of resistence.

According to the estimate of the union leader Carl Severing, over one thousand workers were killed during the fighting against the counter-revolutionaries, or were shot after being captured. Eighteen months after the coup 412 persons accused of supporting the Kapp putsch had been amnestied; only one person had been sentenced – to five years imprisonment (Walter Tormin, *Die Weimarer Republik*, Hannover 1973, p. 110). In the national elections held on 6 June 1920 the SPD vote crashed by almost half. The Independents raised their share of the vote from 7.6 per cent to 18 per cent, with the Communists

liberated, and when Essen fell to the Red Army after four days of intense fighting the workers seemed to have achieved a great victory.

But the fruits of victory were bitter indeed. On 17 March, seeing that the coup had been effectively countered by the General Strike, Kapp fled to Sweden. On 20 March the government returned to Berlin and issued a call to go back to work, although this got under way only after the strike leaders successfully demanded the resignation of Noske. Hence, overnight, the disloyal army units in the Ruhr, still under von Watter's command, became the legitimate agents of an elected government. The Red Army was suddenly confronting not putschists but government soldiers, and right-wing *Reichswehr* units were being assembled in Bavaria to

1. The Workers

While the fighting raged in the Ruhr, Paul Loebe reported that the cabinet's greatest worry was that 'the Reichswehr might be annhilated, and that there would be no protection against Spartacists and plunderers' (cabinet sitting, 12 March 1920).

gaining a further 2 per cent, while the right-wing parties all lost support to the liberal centre parties. The election demonstrated a massive vote of no confidence in the Majority Socialists, and represented a major swing to the left in German politics. Yet two weeks later a new minority government of centre and centre-right parties was formed to replace the previous centre-left coalition. It was the first time since the November Revolution that the SPD was out of power.

The Munich Workers' Republic

The pattern of political developments in Berlin and the Ruhr very much dominated the experience of the first three years of the Weimar Republic. Indeed many of the broad political conflicts of the time – centralised parliamentary democracy or grass-roots council democracy, a people's militia or a national army – were expressed in a remarkably similar fashion across the country, in spite of great variations in local conditions. But one area of Germany, isolated in many respects both geographically and culturally from the rest of the nation, experienced acutely the upheaval set off by the collapse of the old order. This was Bavaria, an essentially rural Catholic state in southern Germany, where revolution and counter-revolution mixed political passion and personal tragedy with the element of farce.

The Socialist Republic of Bavaria came into being on the night of 7 November 1918 – nearly forty-eight hours before the republic was proclaimed in Berlin. In fact, the example of this perfectly executed *coup d'état* against the Bavarian monarchy accelerated the development of the revolution in the capital itself. Yet from the outset the case of Bavaria was unique. Events unfolded there in isolation from the

A demonstration of ex-soldiers outside the Foreign Office in Munich demands work and proper pensions for war-invalids.

rest of Germany, and the common cultural identity shared by the Bavarian people facilitated a specifically 'Bavarian' experiment in political government.

The leader of the Bavarian radicals, Kurt Eisner, was a man of exceptional talent if not always predictable temperament. Essentially an intellectual who felt ill-at-ease among politicians, he was the antithesis of those Social Democratic leaders who had worked their way up from the factory floor. As a result, the Independent Socialist group which gathered around this Prussian Jew attracted an unlikely combination of soldiers, poets, writers and philosophers – a mixture which even found expression in one individual: the dramatist, poet and Red Guard commander Ernst Toller.

Despite the Independents' lack of a firm political base, even among the workers of Munich, Eisner's group came to dominate the first post-war Bavarian government, because of its coalition with the Majority Social Democrats. Despite his utopian beliefs, Eisner himself was a realist, and the first government attempted only cautious reforms. Indeed it was Eisner who coined the phrase, much repeated by politicians without his integrity or humanity, 'we cannot proceed with the socialisation of the economy at present, since there is nothing left to socialise'. In Munich, as elsewhere, conflicts soon developed between the system of Soldiers' and Workers' Councils and the principle of a National Assembly. Though Eisner saw the councils as an ideal instrument for the participation of the 'common man' in the task of government, he sought a solution to the conflict by proposing a dual system of local and national assemblies. Such a compromise was just sufficient to maintain his fragile coalition with the Majority Socialists, who could offer no viable alternative to his popular leadership. Yet in effect Eisner's personality was the only link holding together the radicals and the SPD, and as tensions grew in the first half of February 1919 he announced his

intention to resign and form an official opposition in the Bavarian parliament. On 21 February he left his residence to walk to the assembly and present his resignation, only to be accosted in the street by a nationalist fanatic, Anton Graf Arco auf Valley, and shot dead.

Eisner's murder set off a chain reaction. Incensed workers took to the streets protesting at what they saw as 'bourgeois terrorism'. Thinking that they could revenge Eisner's death, two workers rushed into the Bavarian Assembly and shot dead a deputy and an army major. The parliament dissolved in panic, and in the ensuing power vacuum an executive committee of Soldiers' and Workers' Councils took over the task of government. A final attempt to create a government based upon the Bavarian Assembly was made in mid-March under the leadership of the SPD minister Johannes Hoffmann; but when this cabinet showed itself incapable of tackling major political issues, the Independent Socialists unilaterally declared Munich to be a Workers' Republic (*Räterepublic*) based on the power of the Workers' and Soldiers' Councils. The Communist Party, for once under the leadership of a highly capable Berlin party worker, by the name of Eugen Leviné, immediately withdrew their support, claiming the enterprise to be suicidal. Even a number of the Independent Socialist leaders were sceptical of the undertaking. But the die was cast, and however hopeless the situation may have seemed to the left-wing leaders, the rank and file seemed determined to prove the 'honour' of the Bavarian proletariat. Leviné was under no illusions about the likely fate of the republic, but he eventually took over its leadership and determined to turn imminent defeat into a propaganda victory for the workers' cause.

Announcing that 'the will of the masses and of the Soldiers' and Workers' Councils is the rock on which we must build', Leviné acted decisively. Political prisoners were set free; the Councils took over day-to-day

Eugen Leviné. Born in 1883 in St Petersberg (Leningrad) Leviné was educated at boarding school in Germany. He took part in the Russian Revolution of 1905, was arrested, imprisoned and finally exiled to Siberia where he worked in a lead mine. He escaped from Russia, and later studied economics at Heidelberg university. After serving in the German armed forces during the war, he worked in the Rheinland and Upper Silesia, before being sent to Munich by the Berlin Communist Party after Eisner's murder. A brilliant organiser and inspiration to those around him, Leviné was often torn by self-doubt and lacked the ruthlessness required of a successful revolutionary leader.

Revolution in München. Waffenausgabe an die Arbeiter-Wehr am Marsfeld.

DIRIGIBLE BALLOON

Above The Red Guard 'Air Defence Squadron' assembles on the Marsfeld.

Below Red Guards outside government buildings, April 1919.

1. The Workers

government; the workers were armed and a Red Guard formed; luxury flats were expropriated and given to the homeless; and factories were run by joint councils of workers and owners (when the latter had not fled). For many Bavarians the millennium had arrived! The minister in charge of finance announced that capitalist exploitation was a product of the 'money economy' and telegraphed the Central Bank in Berlin to demand the abolition of paper currency in favour of universal exchange. At the Ministry for Bavarian Affairs a steady stream of callers offered their advice on everything from alchemy to truffle-farming, while the Minister for Culture played host to a series of individuals, each convinced that he held the key to the 'universal happiness of man'.

But an armed ring was closing round Munich. Although an attempted counter-revolution was foiled by Red Guards, Free-corps units were massing on Bavaria's northern borders. Attempts to reach an accord with the 'official' Hoffmann government in Bamberg failed. A wave of atrocity propaganda was unleashed against the Workers' Republic, which encouraged the advancing mercenaries to behave as an invading army. When three Red Cross workers were executed in Possendorf for tending wounded Red Guardists, wild rumours began to sweep Munich that the soldiers were under order to massacre the revolutionaries. The atmosphere of panic overturned the careful preparations of the Republic's leaders, with tragic results. The order for the Red Army to disband was ignored by many workers, who had no intention of dying without a fight. And on the night of 29 April, eight hostages were shot in the Luitpold Gymnasium after a self-styled court martial had found them guilty of being right-wing spies.

The shooting was a criminal act, and all those involved were later executed. But the atrocity provided justification for a reign of white terror in Munich, which even according to official figures claimed the

The Freecorps 'Werdenfels' in full Bavarian costume march into Munich on 1 May 1919. In fact the Freecorps generals did not dare to use Bavarian troops against the Munich Red Guard for fear that they would prove unreliable. Instead Prussian soldiers (with their historical dislike for Bavarians) carried out all 'military duties'.

Above Self-appointed 'bourgeois vigilantes' lead away suspected revolutionaries after the entry of Freecorps troops into the centre of Munich.

Left Freecorps troops proudly display a prisoner shortly before his execution (the photograph was taken by the Lieutenant in charge of the firing squad).

lives of 557 men and women between 1 and 8 May. In fact independent estimates suggest that over 700 were killed ('Zwei Jahre Mord', E. Gumbel, Berlin 1921). The massacre only ended when twenty-one young students were summarily executed after being denounced as Red soldiers by a school caretaker. In fact they were all members of a Catholic seminary group meeting to discuss theology.

Leviné himself was arrested and charged with high treason and complicity in the murder of the hostages. As leader of the Workers' Republic, he accepted full responsibility for the murder, though he refused to state whether he had known of the decision to execute the hostages. His defiant last speech to the court provoked an uproar, and for a time it seemed that

The official caption to this press photograph read:

'The Württemberg Freecorps give up their midday meal to starving children in Munich's poorest quarter.'

It was in the proletarian quarter that the massacres of suspected revolutionaries took place.

the military authorities would not dare execute him, in view of the threat of a nationwide strike. A telegram was sent from the central government asking for the death sentence to be commuted to imprisonment. But somehow it arrived an hour after the firing squad had done its work. The legal inquiry into the circumstances leading to the murder of the hostages reported three months later. Leviné was completely exonerated.

The hostages were all members of the *Thule-Bund*, a secret anti-Semitic organisation dedicated to the 'eradication' of Jewish influence in Germany. Members of the *Thule-Bund* helped form the German Workers Party (DAP), which became the German National Socialist Workers Party (NSDAP) under the leadership of Adolf Hitler.

The German Communist Party

The Third International

Shortly after the founding of the German Communist Party in December 1918, overtures reached Berlin from the new Bolshevik regime in Moscow, proposing the creation of a new organisation to replace the now discredited Second International of the pre-war Social Democratic parties. In the final days of her life, Rosa Luxemburg expressed hostility to such a development, not only because of her various political differences with Lenin and the Bolsheviks, but because she feared that a new International, without the counterweight of a mass-based European Communist party, would in time fall under the influence of the Soviet party apparatus. And even when, on 24 January 1919, the founding congress of the Third (Communist) International took place in Moscow (the Third International became known as the Communist International or 'Comintern'), the German delegate Hugo Eberlain continued to express his party's opposition to the move. In the interests of unity, however, Eberlain refrained from voting against the formation of the new International body, and the KPD accepted the majority's will.

The patriarchal attitude of the Russian leaders to the other European parties soon became apparent. The KPD was a small, largely ineffectual and frequently distrusted element of the German labour movement – a victim as much of its own inept strategy as of the Majority Socialists' vilification. The Kapp putsch, and the KPD's undisciplined reponse to it, convinced Lenin that the party held a weak and exposed position among the vanguard of the German workers. One solution to this problem was to attract the more progressive elements of the Independent Socialists to the Communist camp, and with this in mind the Comintern invited a delegation from the USPD to attend their Second Congress.

At this time the KPD was led by Paul Levi, an able and articulate lawyer and a firm disciple of Rosa Luxemburg; a man who, though hardly renowned for cutting a heroic proletarian image, was none the less an intellectual of independent mind. The Second Congress took place in an atmosphere of high expectation. The Red Army, having almost crushed the power of the White forces in Russia, was advancing across Poland and could be expected to stand on the eastern frontier of Germany within a matter of days. Lenin in particular read the situation with unaccustomed optimism, expecting a second wave of revolution to spread out from central Europe towards the west. Levi, however, was decidedly sceptical about the immediate prospects of revolution in western Europe, and clashed frequently with the Russian leadership. But in the elation of the moment his position was weak, and the Second Congress affirmed the principle that the parties affiliated to the Third International must become a 'single communist movement having branches in different countries'.

The USPD delegation left Moscow deeply divided about accepting the twenty-one conditions which the Comintern had attached to membership, and Levi returned to Germany distrustful of Russian influence on the future course of European communism. On 12 October 1920 a special congress was called by the Independent Socialists to discuss the twenty-one conditions, and thereby the possibility of amalgamation with the KPD. After a long and acrimonious debate, the delegates voted by 236 votes to 156 to accept. This decision led to an influx of some 300,000 USPD members into the KPD, and in December an Unification Congress took place in Berlin to inaugurate the new era of mass action which this merger promised. The new party was now some 350,000 strong. But its strength was a result of Comintern policies, not of internal growth and consolidation, while the independent spirit of Rosa Luxemburg was alive only in her portraits, which covered the walls of the congress hall. Two months later, in February 1921, Levi was ousted from the leadership of the party because of his opposition to the Comintern's policy towards the Italian Socialist Party, and the leadership of the KPD passed into the hands of leaders of bureaucratic ability but pedestrian intellect. The results of this purge of the so-called 'rightist' leadership exploded a few weeks later in the March Action.

The March Action

During the early months of 1921 Germany lurched from one crisis to another, not only as a result of internal political conflict, but also because of the perilous state of relations with the allies over reparations and disarmament. On 7 March the French and Belgian governments ordered the occupation of the cities of Duisberg, Düsseldorf and Ruhrort in retaliation for Germany's failure to deliver reparation payments. Simultaneously, demands that Bavarian para-military forces be disbanded in line with the agreement restricting the numbers of military forces in Germany provoked another crisis of confidence in the leadership of the republic. All in all, a new wave of radical unrest seemed about to sweep the country, and the Communist leadership expected revolutionary sentiments to ride on the crest of that wave.

The exact origins and the circumstances surrounding the March Action are still a matter of controversy and conjecture. It appears that representatives of the Comintern arrived in Germany at the beginning of March, among them Bela Kun. What is not clear is who gave them their orders – an inner clique of the Comintern acting without authority, or the Bolshevik leadership itself. Certainly Bela Kun would appear to have had a hand in organising events, unknown to many German activists, although his precise movements are difficult to trace. Plans were laid for a General Strike in central Germany after the Easter holidays, and preparation for armed action went ahead accordingly. But unexpected events short-circuited these preparations after an unsuccessful bomb attack was carried out in Berlin. Claiming that the group responsible was based in Saxony, the government ordered a security sweep of the Eisleben, Mansfeld and Meresburg areas by members of a special police squad. Although it was announced that the sweep was a limited 'anti-crime' operation, the forces involved were clearly out of all proportion to such a task. Indeed it may have been an attempt to provoke or anticipate a suspected Communist uprising – a theory later given credence by Minister Severing's statement in the Prussian Diet.

Whatever the truth of the matter, the KPD action went off prematurely and ineffectively, using the police action as a pretext for insurrection. Although many workers did respond by striking and occupying mines and factories, the action was condemned by the greater part of the

Max Holz (centre with binoculars) during the March Events in central Germany.

labour movement and its leaders. Only the legendary Max Holz, a radical guerilla leader of great panache and daring but sadly limited schooling in the disciplines of revolutionary socialism, was able to inspire the workers' confidence. His band, armed with weapons stored after earlier battles in the Ruhr, roamed the region without any clearly defined aim or strategic plan and only a minimum of military discipline. Moreover Holz was totally deaf to the demands of the Communist leadership that the uprising should be organised from party headquarters. After hiding in a mine shaft, being arrested and then escaping disguised as a travelling egg-salesman, he was eventually captured and sent to Berlin, where his trial became a political and social sensation. The fate of most rank and-file Communists and workers was less romantic. When the March Action was finally called off by the KPD Central Committee, 145 workers had been killed, hundreds wounded and 3,470 taken prisoner.

The March Action was a severe set-back for the German Communist Party, and the grass roots membership passed their own verdict on the competence of the leadership when nearly half the party deserted during the summer months. Conditions had also changed in Russia. The crushing of the Kronstadt mutiny in mid-March and the introduction of the New Economic Policy signified the need to find some mode of accommodation with the outside world through a series of trade agreements and political treaties. The German fiasco strengthened Lenin's thesis that a temporary retreat on the revolutionary front was inevitable, and Comintern policy was soon signalling this approach. The rallying cry to emerge from the Third Congress of the Communist International in July 1921 was 'To the masses!', and splits in the German party were (temporarily) smoothed over, not by the bullying tactics which Stalin was later to employ, but by the careful teamwork of Lenin, Trotsky and Zinoviev. Even so, the dependence of the KPD on Moscow's guidance was to be a chronic source of weakness for the development of German Communism once the internecine struggle within the Bolshevik leadership sharpened after Lenin's death.

'To the masses'

During the next eighteen months the KPD underwent a succession of internal crises and leadership struggles as the consequences of the abortive March Action worked themselves out. The strategic question was whether capitalism was on the decline or whether it was consolidating and holding its own in the aftermath of the November Revolution and the civil war. The policy of 'To the masses!' presupposed the building of a united front with the reformist wing of the labour movement. So should the KPD retain its character as a small, sectarian Bolshevik-style organisation, actively preparing to seize power in a revolutionary struggle, or should it become a mass-based democratic party acting as the nucleus of all radical and

progressive forces on the left? Early in 1922 the proponents of the latter thesis were expelled from the KPD as 'revisionists'; it was the second major purge in nine months and it was intended to eliminate 'right-wing opportunists'. In effect it silenced those voices who had frequently embarrassed both the KPD's Central Committee and the Comintern with public criticisms of party policy.

In April 1922 Russia and Germany, the two pariah nations of Europe, signed the Rapallo Treaty, agreeing to resume diplomatic relations and laying the groundwork for limited economic and military co-operation. This agreement considerably complicated the relationship between the Soviet leadership and the German Communists, since the interests of Russian foreign policy were now inextricably linked to the internal strategy of the KPD.

On 24 June Germany's Foreign Minister, Walter Rathenau, was murdered by a right-wing death squad, presumably in revenge for signing the treaty with the Soviet Union. Rathenau was yet one more victim of orchestrated right-wing violence which, between 1918 and 1922, accounted for the murders of 354 persons. But Rathenau's assassination triggered a wave of revulsion and anger within the German labour movement, and did much to bring together its various factions in condemnation of the administration's feeble response to right-wing terror. At the same time the endemic economic and political instability which characterised 1922 and 1923, combined with hard proselytising, enabled the KPD to recover most of the ground it had lost in 1921. Moreover, though the 'right-revisionists' had been expelled from the party, the new Central Committee had no intention of burning its fingers again, and in consequence the leadership combined united-front tactics with a healthy caution, refusing to be drawn into premature adventures. Such caution, however, inevitably drew the scorn of left radicals within the party, especially those grouped around Ruth

Fischer and the Berlin party organisation, who saw in the looming currency crisis of 1923 every reason for pressing a more revolutionary line.

1923 – a revolutionary situation?

The occupation of the Ruhr by French and Belgian troops, and the collapse of the German currency when the government ordered a policy of passive resistance led to renewed political and class polarisation (this issue is dealt with in greater detail in Chapter 2). In fact hyper-inflation had been a latent threat to the republic since 1918, but in mid April (1923) the German mark collapsed, and by August the exchange rate stood at four-and-a-half million marks to the American dollar. A few benefited spectacularly from the Great Inflation; in particular those bankers, industrialists and currency speculators who were able to deal in foreign currency or real estate. For the vast majority, however,

During 1923 workers faced a bitter struggle for survival as hyper-inflation and an employers' offensive against the trade unions forced down real wages and depressed living standards. *Above* Queues form at midday outside a soup-kitchen in Berlin: for the elderly and the unemployed this was often the only meal of the day. *Below*. A worker's family at the table. By 1924 real wages had dropped to 74 per cent of the average level in 1913.

'… Very many children, even the youngest, never taste a drop of milk and come to school with no food inside them … many have no shirt or warm clothing, or else are kept away from class because they have no underwear … (as a result) all they can think about is the struggle against cold and hunger' (Report by the Mayor of Berlin, 1922).

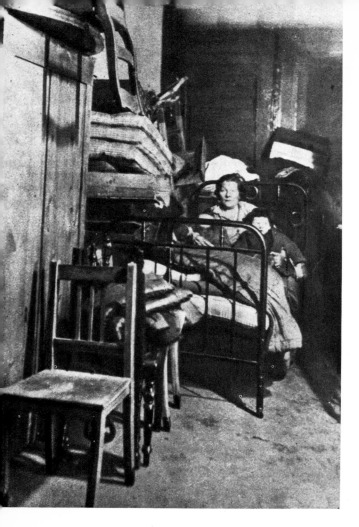

seemed that the economy might actually collapse. The strike movement spread rapidly throughout Berlin, crippling the municipal electricity system, transport, construction and even the hospitals. Again the Communists found themselves chasing the strike movement, rather than organising or leading it. When at last the KPD did manage to exert its influence, it was too late. The sudden resignation of the Cuno government on 12 August, and its replacement by Stresemann's Great Coalition – a coalition which included four SPD ministers – did much to dampen the genuinely revolutionary ardour of the masses which had been deepening during the spring and summer of 1923. Even so, the political atmosphere remained highly volatile, especially in view of the hostility to Stresemann's coalition of many workers normally loyal to the SPD. Stresemann had, after all, been an outspoken annexionist during the Great War, and he was a champion of the German People's Party – hardly a friend of the working class.

The KPD did try to prolong the strike movement after the announcement of the Great Coalition, but the party's all too frequent changes of political direction and

A woman and her two children squat in the hallway of a Berlin apartment block after being evicted from their home because of rent arrears.

During 1923 there were 2,162 major industrial disputes, involving at one time 1,824,000 workers either on strike or locked out by the employers. In total 14,584,000 days were lost through such action (in 1926 there were 383 disputes and 1,325,000 days lost). *Below* Strike-pickets outside a coalmine in Mansfeld.

hyper-inflation meant an equally spectacular slide into poverty. In an attempt to defend living standards, workers had to engage in a bitter war of attrition with their employers, who attempted to exploit the financial crisis to demolish the last few gains of the November Revolution – most obviously the eight-hour day.

By early August the economy was in near chaos. On 10 August government printers went on strike in Berlin. No new money could be printed at a time when the purchase of even a few potatoes demanded a bag-full of old currency, and for a time it

its general lack of political vision regarding the non-Communist workers' movement, left it chasing revolutionary phantoms. At the heart of the dilemma was the party's unresolved attitude towards its own political role, and its resultant swings from 'revolution' to 'reformism'. Just as the spectre of the Russian Revolution ever haunted the SPD's attitude towards radical elements within the working class, so the heroic image of that same revolution consistently blinded the leadership of the KPD to the historical differences between Germany and Russia. Thus, even when the German Communists pursued a united front policy in line with the political demands of the moment, the policy was too often conducted in bad faith. And although the faces on the KPD's Central Committee might come and go, it was the German workers who ultimately paid the price for the irrelevant, or Machiavellian, policies which emanated from the Comintern. This dependence upon outside leadership provoked another, and in retrospect the final, Communist attempt to exploit the internal crisis of Weimar Germany during the 1920s.

The German October

Soviet leaders had been following events in Germany during 1923 with eager anticipation, though expectation of Lenin's death now hung over all political deliberations in Moscow. Still, viewed from the remoteness of the Kremlin, a German revolution seemed inevitable, and in early September Trotsky and Zinoviev summoned Heinrich Brandler to Moscow. Brandler, the new leader of the KPD, was not at all convinced of the prospects for imminent revolution, but in the course of the next four weeks his initial doubts were worn down by the atmosphere of keen expectancy. It is difficult to determine whether the decision to 'name a date' for the German revolution was a result of the struggle for succession within the Bolshevik party. But although the origins of the decision may be disputed, it was certainly decided to prepare for an uprising some time in October or November.

Saxony, with its radical proletarian tradition, was chosen as the jumping-off point for the venture, mainly because there was a chance that the Communists could form a coalition government with the left-wing Social Democrat, Erich Zeigner. After difficult negotiations, a Saxony government was formed on 12 October which included Communist ministers of finance and economics; but the KPD failed to secure the Interior Ministry – and hence control of the armouries of the state police. Zeigner himself, although not the most astute of politicians, was a man of courage and principle, and his project of creating a democratic workers' government was based upon the foundation of 'republican and proletarian defence'. The programme he outlined contained two key clauses. First, Saxony was to be a bulwark against the forces of reaction; proletarian defence forces known as the Proletarian Hundreds were to be formed to protect the government, particularly against the ultra-right based in Bavaria. Secondly, the new government was to represent the interests of the downtrodden and dispossessed against the barons of heavy industry, during a period of widespread unemployment, poverty and hunger.

The day after the formation of the Saxony coalition the national government (in the face of considerable opposition) secured an Enabling Bill which allowed for the imposition of military rule throughout the Reich. General Müller, commander of the Saxony military district, immediately issued an order banning the Proletarian Hundreds or any similar organisation. When Zeigner protested against this order, Müller (acting without consent from Berlin) placed the state police under the control of the army and issued an ultimatum to the Saxon government to submit to his authority. Müller was ably supported in his stand by the bankers of Dresden, who refused a loan of 150 million

41

Despite the debacle of the 'German October', the intense social and political polarisation provoked by the events of 1923 led to a radicalisation of working-class opinion. In national elections held in May 1924 the KPD gained 62 seats in the Reichstag (previously it held only four) while the SPD returned only 100 members compared to a previous total of 172. *Above* A Communist propaganda-lorry during the Presidential election of 1925.

gold marks to the Saxon government to alleviate the crippling food shortage in the region. What the bankers refused the legal government they offered to General Müller. In response, Zeigner's government arranged a trade deal with Russia which exchanged industrial goods for 20,000 tons of grain.

On 20 October Reichswehr troops marched into Saxony – their purpose, according to the central government, being to 'protect the region against attack from secessionist right-wing forces in Bavaria'! In fact the Stresemann government had not dared to risk an army intervention in Bavaria where the right-wing government was in open constitutional rebellion. Instead, Stresemann moved to suppress the left in Saxony in the hope that this

would appease the far-right, and strengthen his hand if he should be forced into the uncomfortable position of asking the Reichswehr to restore Berlin's authority in Bavaria.

General Müller's intervention caught the KPD unprepared for the sudden collapse of the coalition government and with their plans for an uprising far from complete. On the other hand, the army's action incensed the workers and offered an ideal platform on which the radicals could make a stand. Once more, however, the Communist leadership sank to the occasion. At the Chemnitz Conference called to discuss a possible General Strike against the suppression of a democratic government, the KPD's clumsy and over-hasty reaction provoked suspicions that the Communists were about to exploit the situation for their own ends. Fearing that another debacle was in store for the workers, the SPD leadership withdrew its support, and with it that of the major unions. In the words of the veteran communist August Thalheimer, it was a 'third-class funeral'. In the light of their inability to carry even the Saxon working class the KPD's careful

The bitter experience of the first five years of the Weimar Republic left the German workers deeply divided between sympathy for a 'revolutionary' solution to the problem of creating a just and democratic society and those who favoured an attempt to reform the existing status quo. In turn this dilemma mirrored the split in working-class opinion between support for the Communist Party and traditional loyalty to the Social Democrats. The KPD in particular created a close-knit organisation among radical workers which extended solidarity to all those involved in industrial and political disputes with powerful employers' organisations. *Above* The Communist-dominated *Internationale Arbeiterhilfe* (International Workers Aid) distributes groceries to striking textile workers in Oelnitz, Vogtland, in 1927. The slogan on the banner reads, 'Proletarian solidarity will help to free the world'.

preparations for a 'German October' were rendered meaningless. At a hastily called conference the Central Committee agreed that no uprising could be risked in the immediate future. Only in Hamburg was an uprising attempted – a futile and bloody episode whose origins are still far from clear.

Many independent radicals believed that a revolutionary situation genuinely existed during the late summer of 1923. What is certain is that the opportunity for the German working class to take the offensive against its enemies was lost. By the end of the 1920s the forces opposing any form of socialist society had consolidated and entrenched, and by 1930 they were able to carry the attack to the democratic structures of the Weimar state. So, even before the onset of the Great Depression, the German working class was forced on to the defensive to protect even the limited social reforms of the November Revolution. Moreover the bitter legacy of the revolution and the civil war was to debilitate the left in its response to the onslaught of the Nazi party after 1930 – an enemy far more deadly than the forces of 'reaction'.

2

The Middle Class

There was once a nanny-goat who said,
In my cradle someone sang to me:
'A strong man is coming.
He will set you free!'

The ox looked at her askance.
Then turning to the pig
He said,
'That will be the butcher.'

(Bertolt Brecht)

The forming of the Mittelstand

Germany arrived late at the stage of industrial capitalism. Her isolation from the
trade routes to Africa and the New World,
the devastation caused by the Thirty Years
War and her late national unification in
1871 were factors which contributed to this
delayed development. During the last
three decades of the nineteenth century,
however, she passed from being a con-
glomeration of small, largely rural states,
to become the most advanced industrial
nation in Europe. Starting after both
Britain and France, the German Reich had
surpassed her European competitors by the
beginning of the twentieth century in the
production of pig-iron, chemicals and
electric power. Whereas in 1870 Germany
could claim only 13 per cent of the world's
manufactured output compared with
England's 32 per cent, in 1913 she led
England by 16 per cent to 14 per cent
(*Sachwörterbuch der Geschichte
Deutschlands*, Berlin 1969, Bd. 1, p. 807).

The pace of German industrialisation
was therefore extremely rapid, and
technical innovation, which in Britain and
France had been introduced over the
period of a century, came to Germany in
the space of twenty years. More important,
political developments did not keep pace
with the rapid social changes. The autocratic elite which ruled Germany in 1914
was an alliance of feudal Junker land-
owners and industrial 'barons' who exalted
militarism and the Prussian spirit, and
hated liberalism like sin. The middle class
could be distinguished only because it was
neither upper-class nor working-class – a
fact reflected in the term the *Mittelstand*,
meaning a 'middle-estate'. Many of the
Mittelstand were poorer than skilled
industrial workers, though they fiercely
defended their independence as artisans or
small peasant farmers, both fearing and
despising the working class with their
ungodly Marxist beliefs and their lack of
'nationalist spirit'. Naturally, as
industrialisation gathered speed, a 'new'
Mittelstand also came into being, made up
of clerical workers, professionals and
technicians who were more modern and
liberal in outlook than the 'old' *Mittelstand*. Even so, as Germany entered the
second decade of the twentieth century,
both the ruling class and the middle class
contained many elements which properly
belonged to a pre-industrial society.

The resilience of these feudal remnants

in what was essentially a capitalist economy can be partly explained by the fact that Germany experienced no liberal bourgeois revolution, such as had been inaugurated by the English Civil War or the Jacobite Revolution in France. True, there were attempts during the nineteenth century to overthrow the autocratic monarchies of the Federation of German states, but the revolution of 1848 which attempted to achieve national unity in the name of liberal democracy was defeated by the bayonets of the Prussian army. When unification was finally achieved in 1871 it was brought about by Bismarck and the military might of Prussia. Hence the king of Prussia was crowned the 'Kaiser of the German Reich', and although many of the individual states retained their royal dynasties, autocratic Prussia became the dominant state of the new kingdom.

So Germany entered the twentieth century as a rigidly authoritarian society, in which the *Mittelstand* played a grandiose role, patronised politically by the imperial order, protected economically from the harsh reality of free competition by a system of controlled production and distribution, and, in matters of culture, profoundly nationalistic and reactionary. The ambition of every aspiring *petit bourgeois* male was to gain a minor commission in the army, and live out a comfortable existence secure in his status as an officer in a society obsessed with the decorum and bravado of military life.

The First World War and its legacy

The middle classes greeted the outbreak of war in 1914 with unrestrained enthusiasm. But those not conscripted into the armed forces quickly found that a war economy was no respecter of social pride. Modern warfare demanded modern and rational methods of production. Industry was favoured at the expense of agriculture, while large firms were favoured at the

'The ambition of every aspiring petit bourgeois male was to gain a minor commission in the army ... in a society obsessed with the decorum and bravado of military life.' Members of the German armed forces pose outside a German Beer Restaurant in Lille, France, during the First World War.

expense of small workshops or individual handicraft workers who had neither the capital nor the expertise to produce howitzers, mustard gas, or phosphorous shells. Many small producers, unable to gain either government contracts or raw materials, which were severely rationed, were forced to close their businesses and enter the munition factories as manual labourers. While production in the war industries doubled or tripled, textile production in 1918 was only 17 per cent of its pre-war total and house-building had declined to 4 per cent.

For the small businessman the war meant ruin and often proletarianisation. For the large industrialists, such as Krupp and Bosch, it spelt rapid expansion and massive profit. Indeed a substantial impulse to war had been the desire to expand the market for German goods in Europe, in view of Germany's failure to gain an extensive colonial empire and a subsequent outlet for its exports. (At the outbreak of the First World War Germany controlled an empire one tenth the size of Great Britain's, with a mere 12.3 million inhabitants compared with the British Empire's 393.5 million. The European market accounted for 75 per cent of Germany's exports compared with 35 per cent of Britain's.) It is therefore no surprise to find that the war aims of the German government in 1914 were directed towards three specific goals: first the expansion of a German sphere of influence in Europe, primarily at the expense of its main rival France; secondly, access to French and Belgian Channel ports, and thereby a highway to world trade; and thirdly, the expansion of a colonial empire in Africa and the East (see p. 3).

But Germany's great military gamble failed. Rarely, however, did those in the trenches discover that the war had indeed been lost on the battlefield. The officer corps in particular believed the myth, put around by the old ruling class, that the left-wing parties were responsible for Germany's defeat by 'stabbing her in the back' when victory was at hand. Return-ing home from the front was a bitter experience. There were no waving crowds welcoming home a victorious army. Instead it was the hated working class who seemed to be in control. Military insignia, the flag of the fatherland and 'proper morals' – everything that represented German middle-class life before the war – were now denigrated. In their place a regime which preached egality, brotherhood and internationalism was taking shape. The parallel with Russia seemed incontestable.

Unveeringly hostile to what they saw as Bolshevism, many young middle-class soldiers joined the Freecorps, which provided not only an essential means of earning a living, but also a violent outlet for their frustrations and political ideals. Others joined war-veterans' associations, such as the Stahlhelm, which attempted to revive Wilhelmian virtues in the new republic. Even so, 'red workers' were not the only object of hate for uprooted members of the old *Mittelstand*. Big business too was regarded as evil, for while hundreds of thousands had experienced the war in the trenches, those in the board-rooms and in society salons had grown fat on the speculation in death. Small family businesses had collapsed, while big business expanded and prospered. A middle-class revolutionary spirit, equally hostile to the Stock Exchange and

A lieutenant describes his reactions on his return to Germany:

We sat in our bunkers and heard about the mess behind the lines, about the dry rot setting in back home ... We felt that the Frenchmen and the Tommies were no longer our worst enemies, that there was worse to come, real poison was being brewed in the witches' cauldron at home ... The march home was my most bitter experience ... I was a broken man who could no longer find God and who was about to lose himself ... from blood, muck and misery we returned. But when we glimpsed Germany the ground under our feet began to sink.

(Peter Merkl, *Political Violence under the Swastika*, Princeton 1975, p. 55)

Otto Braun (MSPD) remembers his first day in Office as Prussian Minister for Agriculture in November 1918.

The secretary of state announced that the ministerial civil servants had assembled to meet me. In the conference room they were packed together like sardines ... in their faces a mixture of hate, defiance and mistrustful curiosity. Nowhere any feeling which might have betrayed the slightest sympathy for the new regime. Many of them had assisted their Minister or represented him in the Reichstag, and were used to looking down their noses at us Social Democratic members, the 'plebs' in the three-class parliament.

(O.Braun, *Von Weimar zu Hitler*, Hamburg 1949)

Marxism, began to flourish in the post-war months.

The lost war and the only half-fulfilled revolution created a political stalemate in Germany. The organised power of the labour movement was sufficient to win substantial reforms from big business: an agreement on the eight-hour day and the commitment to free collective bargaining. And although these gains were gradually whittled away over the next few years, the old ruling class was unable to win back its pre-war position of supremacy, as the collapse of the Kapp putsch demonstrated. Yet the failure of the Social Democrat and liberal parties to consolidate parliamentary democracy by a thorough purge and reform of the military, the judiciary and the bureaucracy, and their unwillingness to socialise key industries, left powerful enclaves of authoritarianism and anti-republicanism at large within the Weimar state. The old *Mittelstand* was therefore in a no-man's land between the two warring factions of German society. Under the empire the middle classes had traded off support for the *status quo* in return for economic protection and social status. The collapse of the German domestic economy under the impact of war and the economic dislocation which followed stripped away that protection and exposed the *Mittel-*

stand to the harsh winds of competition from large conglomerate companies with modern production techniques. Social prestige also proved to be an ephemeral quality, particularly for those unable to keep up appearances in salon society. But of all the events which left their mark upon the psyche of the German *Mittelstand*, none was so traumatic as the Great Inflation.

The Great Inflation

The hyper-inflation that raged during 1922 and 1923 and the world economic depression which broke towards the end of 1929 are normally seen as the decisive events which destroyed the fabric of Weimar society and prepared the way for the rise of German fascism. The hyper-inflation was decisive in that it had psychological and political effects far beyond the impact of the actual economic chaos caused by the collapse of the German currency. The Depression was crucial, because it provoked a widespread and bitter class polarisation in German society during a period of political instability.

In order to understand the long-term political effects of the hyper-inflation it is necessary to examine not only how inflation affected different social classes,

48

but equally how the inflation affected the different sections of the middle class. For the inflation finally and spectacularly demonstrated to those members of the *Mittelstand* who considered themselves 'above politics' that political organisation was necessary in order to guarantee their very survival. Even more alarmingly, it demonstrated that the *Mittelstand*, far from being the vital middle estate of society, was in fact an amorphous mass of individuals with few common interests; nor could they rely upon the political parties of the working class or the upper classes to represent their particular economic demands.

The origins of the hyper-inflation

The hyper-inflation had its origins in the general system of finance practised by German industry. Unlike Britain and the USA, where commercial banks acted as sources of credit for the wider financial market, Germany had banks which were originally planned as institutions for the *direct* financing of heavy industry. Funds were mainly used for loans to industrial and commercial customers, and either one bank or a consortium of banks would lend money for projects such as the construction of a steel works, a new mining venture or the building of a chemical refinery. In return, the banks gained the majority of shares issued by the company to finance its expansion. Conversely the general public, instead of investing widely in shares issued on the Stock Exchange, subscribed to government savings bonds.

The relationship between banks and heavy industry naturally became very close, and every major bank had its boardroom connections with at least one branch of heavy industry. This inter-relationship fostered a process of capital concentration, for it became necessary to raise huge sums of capital as industry became increasingly mechanised. Another factor which promoted capital concentration was the status of trusts and cartels

in German law. While in the United States anti-trust laws made the infringement of free competition a criminal offence, in Germany cartel agreements had legal status and could be enforced in the courts. Even in the mid 1890s there were official cartels in iron, steel, coal, cement, plate glass and chemical manufacturing. By 1914 the framework of the German cartel structure was well established, with either rigid or loose systems of production quotas, market sharing and price-fixing agreements. Among small producers the formation of producers' and buyers' co-operatives had much the same effect in severely limiting free competition and legitimising cartel policies.

The war had two major effects on the structure of the German economy. First, as already suggested, the production of armaments at the expense of consumer goods favoured heavy industry and accelerated capital concentration. Secondly, the cost of the war had severely inflationary effects because the government, fearing to harm the interests of its political backers, lacked the will to impose a progressive taxation system. Instead of imposing tax increases upon industry and the wealthy (which was done only belatedly and ineffectually), the authorities attempted to cover the mountain of debt by issuing war bonds. And although the purchase of such bonds by the German public became increasingly less 'voluntary' as the war progressed, the sums so raised never remotely paid for the billions of marks' worth of munitions shot off by the armed forces. The government's reponse was to print more money, and by the end of the war the amount of paper money in circulation had risen six-fold in comparison with 1913.

Hence the German inflation really began in 1914, although its effects were disguised by the closing of the foreign exchanges for the duration of the war and the introduction of rationing. By November 1918 the German mark had declined to half its former gold value on neutral money

Above The skeletons of German warplanes lie in a scrapyard – destroyed as a result of the Versailles Treaty.

Below Huge demonstrations were called in Germany to protest against the conditions attached to the Treaty of Versailles. An SPD delegate addresses the crowd below the 'Iron Hindenberg' in Berlin.

markets, although only after the total collapse of the controlled war economy did the full extent of Germany's economic dislocation become apparent.

The Treaty of Versailles

The peace treaty imposed upon Germany at Versailles by the victorious allies was an impossible burden for a country already crippled by the human and material cost of the war. Germany was forced to cede the vital industrial region of Alsace Lorraine, as well as half Upper Silesia, with its valuable coal and ore deposits. Additionally she was forced to hand over:

all armaments material and battleships;
all merchant ships over 1,600 tons;
half her merchant fleet between 1000 and
    1600 tons;
one quarter of her fishing fleet and one fifth
    of her canal and river fleet;
5,000 locomotives, 150,000 railway wagons
    and 5,000 motor vehicles.

But even this was a mere trifle compared with the astronomical sums demanded by the allies as reparation for war damages, which was fixed at 132 billion gold marks in May 1921. (An amount which the economist John Maynard Keynes reckoned to be three times more than Germany could possibly pay.)

It was because of Germany's alleged failure to pay reparations in full that the French and Belgians invaded the Ruhr in January 1923. When a wave of popular indignation and nationalism swept across Germany in response to this occupation, the government ordered a policy of passive resistance to the French troops whose intention was to 'liberate' massive quantities of coal as payment in kind. Passive resistance merely put an even greater strain upon German's precarious finances, and in the second half of 1923 the mark collapsed against the American dollar and other major currencies:

A French soldier guards a train full of German coal, bound for France as reparation payment.

Jan	1921	64.9 (marks to the dollar)
July	1921	76.7
Jan	1922	191.8
July	1922	493.2
Jan	1923	17,792
July	1923	353,412
August	1923	4,620,455
Sept	1923	98,860,000
Oct	1923	25,260,208,000
Nov	1923	4,200,000,000,000

Initially prices in German shops rose more slowly than the dollar quotation. But by January 1923 the entire nation was painfully aware of the connection between

51

Above Paper money for the payment of wages is collected in washing baskets and sacks from the Reichsbank.

Below At the height of the hyper-inflation paper currency was packed into boxes and sold as waste paper. According to the prices on the board, such 'money' was more valuable than bones, but not as valuable as old rags!

Kaufe:
Stampfpapier: 20,000
Lumpen: 50,000 Mark.
Knochen: 5,000 Mark.

the daily exchange rate and commodity prices. Adjustments soon became a daily, and then a half-daily, occurence. Fresh prices would be chalked up in shops and restaurants as soon as the morning dollar quotation was known. Life became tragi-comic. Anyone with access to even a few dollars or pounds sterling became a trillionaire overnight. But it often proved impossible to change one hundred dollars into German currency, since even the banks did not have enough paper currency available, and anyway it would have required a lorry to transport the money. An unskilled worker who in 1913 had been earning 25 marks per week was earning 530 million marks a week in September 1923; even then he had lost nearly thirty per cent of his previous purchasing power. He would have needed a wheelbarrow to take home his weekly wage. A pensioner who in 1913 invested the regal sum of 100,000 marks (real value approximately 25,000 dollars) would have found his account worth less than a few cents in 1923. The banks usually demanded that such accounts be closed, since the cost of administration was far higher than the value of the savings. A couple who owned a large house before the war and received an income from letting the rooms, would find in 1923 that the cost of replacing a broken pane of glass was more than all the rent they had ever received from their tenants, since the level of rents was fixed, while glass prices were not.

Not everyone was a loser, however. Until January 1922 the Central Reichsbank held its rate of interest at 5 per cent per annum. In August 1923 this was finally raised to 30 per cent, but even in September 1923 it reached a high point of only 90 per cent. It did not require a financial genius to reckon that such interest rates were only a minute percentage of the rate of depreciation, and anyone with direct access to central bank loans could borrow money and pay back with devalued currency. But only large private banks, and hence heavy industry, had access to such borrowing

Hugo Stinnes (left): 'We must have the courage to say to the people, "for the present and for some time to come, you will have to work overtime without any payment" ' (Stinnes to National Economic Council, October 1922).

facilities. Boardroom speculators therefore procured cheap loans and purchased every 'physical' asset available: factories, mines, stocks of raw materials, shops, farms – whatever had a good chance of retaining its real value. They were helped in this process because small firms found credit virtually impossible to obtain, precisely because of the rapid depreciation of the mark, while the cost of new stock was always far higher than the previous day's selling-price. Sections of German industry, in par-

Stinnes as seen by the left wing press in 1922:

> Only the ten-hour day can solve this mess.
> Of course we'll pay the worker less.
>
> Pay reparations – quickly, without pain
> And then – fill our pockets once again
>
> The unemployed out on the streets
> Have nothing now at all to eat.
>
> For the fatherland (and our profits) to bloom
> All, all must meet their doom!

And as portrayed by the Nazis in 1928 as a victim of the Jews (*Der Angriff*, 19 March 1928):

> The mighty Stinnes – eaten up by Jacob
> Goldsmith.

ticular those who could export their goods, experienced a boom of unprecedented proportions. They could undercut competition in foreign markets, while the foreign currency earned from export sales had a highly inflated value inside Germany.

Gigantic fortunes were amassed within a period of a few months. Probably the most notorious of these speculators was the financier Hugo Stinnes who, although a wealthy man before the inflation, used the currency crisis to extend his empire from coalmining to electricity production, banks, hotels, paper mills, newspapers and other publishing ventures. Described by the American Secretary of State for Western Europe, W.R. Castle, as 'the strongest man in Germany … and one of the most dangerous men in the world', Stinnes combined vast political influence with unlimited personal ambition. He was particularly obsessed with what he regarded as the 'threat of world Bolshevism', and conspired behind the scenes to create a German dictator capable of 'speaking the language of the people', who would forcefully reintroduce the ten-hour working day and enable Germany to regain her position of greatness. Stinnes died in April 1924, shortly after the mark was stabilised (and his paper empire collapsed), but his manipulative style of politics was emulated in a less public fashion by many of the leaders of heavy industry during Hitler's rise to power in the late 1920s and early 1930s.

The other section of the population to benefit materially from the hyper-inflation was the landowning class, whether Prussian Junker or small peasant-proprietor. The indebted Prussian land-owners were able to pay off debts on their huge eastern estates with inflated currency, for food crops, like any other physical asset, maintained a real value. In fact, in the final chaotic months of the hyper-inflation, paper currency was largely abandoned, and purchasing took place through direct bartering and exchange

Above Passengers leave Berlin on a so-called 'Hamster-trip' to the countryside ... and (*right*) return laden with potatoes and food exchanged for items of jewelry, household goods and the like.

rather than through money payments. Even the smallest landholders were able to exploit their position as meat and dairy producers, and stories were rife of peasant huts resplendent with pianos and elegant furniture which had been exchanged for a chicken or a dozen eggs by impoverished middle-class city dwellers! Indeed the position of a great many urban *petit bourgeois* families was more abject than that of the workers, for the latter were able to win at least some form of automatic compensation for inflation in their wage packets.

Stabilisation

The 'miracle of the Rentenmark', in essence a clever psychological illusion, put an end to the inflation in November 1923 (the Rentenmark was supposed to derive its value from an assessment of the sum total of national wealth). The government's printing presses were shut down and, helped by the so-called Dawes Plan, which was to bolster the German economy

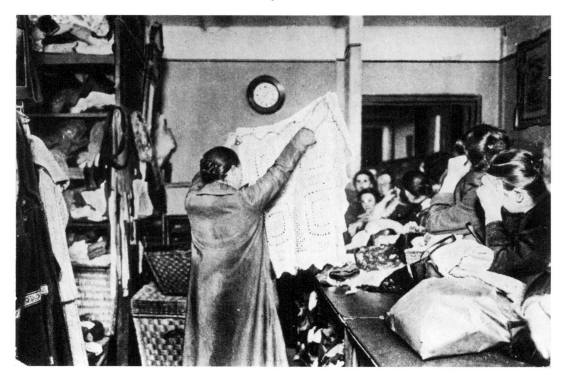

Above Many members of the *Mittelstand* were forced into abject poverty by the hyper-inflation. At a Berlin pawnbroker's women pawn articles of clothing and household linen – often heirlooms that had been in the family for generations.

Below For the few who benefited from the hyper-inflation, advances in technology and mass production meant that afternoon coffee could be taken to the accompaniment of light music from the radio.

by means of capital loans from abroad, life returned to a semblance of normality. The dollar, which was quoted at 2,520 billion marks on 16 November 1923, was quoted at 4.2 Rentenmarks three days later.

There can be no doubt that the intensity and the time scale of the German inflation was greatly increased by the refusal of heavy industry to support stabilisation on anything but the most selfishly advantageous terms, as discussions on 're-valorisation' were to show. For stabilisation meant the bursting of the speculative bubble, as borrowers had to repay loans valued in inflated currency with lower-value Rentenmarks. A new wave of bankruptcies swept the country, and although this also caught out many speculators from the world of high finance, its more drastic effects were felt among medium-sized businesses who lacked foreign capital reserves. A new round of mergers and takeovers followed. By the mid 1920s some 70 per cent of the total capital of all German public companies was in the hands of 2,000 firms. Combines accounted for 93 per cent of turnover in the mining industries, 95 per cent of steel production and 87 per cent of electricity production.

And although rural producers benefited in the short term from the hyper-inflation, it soon became apparent that the traditional foundations of the agricultural economy were beginning to decay as a result of the collapse of the rural credit agencies which had traditionally served the small farmer. By 1927 agriculture was experiencing a crisis as severe as that which gripped the urban *Mittelstand* in 1923.

In response to the inflation all sorts of groups and associations sprang up to protect and represent the interests of those most severely hit: the 'Alliance against Profiteers and Inflation', the 'Protective League of German Mortgagees and Savers', and many others. Their aim was to put an end to the repayment of private loans and mortgages in inflated currency and bring about a revalorisation of those

debts which had been so repaid. But these millions of creditors found themselves confronted by the powerful opposition of the business community, who felt that after stabilisation, the prospects for economic recovery would be seriously damaged by the repayment of revalued debts.

The opponents of revalorisation had their champion in the Finance Minister, Hans Luther, who is generally accepted as the strategist responsible for the stabilisation of the mark. His ties to the financial community and heavy industry meant that stabilisation worked decisively to the advantage of big business and agriculture – precisely those interest groups who had benefited from the inflation – and against the interests of small savers. Not daring to present legislation directly to the Reichstag, Luther used an Enabling Act to force through a bill limiting revalorisation of paper currency debts to 15 per cent of their original gold mark value. Furthermore he exempted the government from the duty to revalue its own debts until outstanding reparations to the Allies had been paid in full – a policy of breathtaking cynicism, considering that one fifth of all public saving was invested in some form of government stock. Finally, any debts that had been repaid even at the height of the

Finance Minister (and later Reichsbank President) Hans Luther (left) in discussion with Heinrich Brüning.

inflation were not subject to any form of revalorisation. Luther's bill became law on 8 December 1923.

The deep-seated bitterness felt by members of the middle classes at the failure of the government to enforce a just revalorisation expressed itself clearly in the May 1924 Reichstag elections. While the working class moved to the left, the *Mittelstand* moved decisively to the right. The German Nationalists (DNVP) and the National Socialist Freedom Movement (an alliance of Nazis and other far-right groups) made considerable gains at the expense of the liberal middle-class parties such as the German Democrats (DDP) and the German People's Party (DVP). More remarkably, a group calling itself the Fighting League of Beggars, representing the new middle-class poor, managed spectacular successes in a number of localities.

However, the German Nationalists quickly abused the trust of their middle-class supporters by joining a national coalition headed by their *bête noir*, Hans Luther himself. So the various revaluation associations, having thrown in their lot with the German Nationalists during the elections, could only watch helplessly as the powerful industrialist lobby within the party blocked all revalorisation proposals which would have guaranteed a high level of revaluation. Although some form of compromise was eventually reached with the middle-class associations, the level of revaluation remained abysmal, and provided for a level of debt restitution of between 5 and 10 per cent. These proposals finally became law in July 1925, but in the process the Nationalist Party was racked by a series of resignations and open splits.

The extent to which hyper-inflation and the subsequent method of stabilisation shook traditional middle-class values and beliefs was demonstrated in 1925, when the various associations of savers and debtors refused to back the Nationalists and other bourgeois parties in condemning the joint socialist and Communist proposal to expropriate the estates of the German princes. They argued that there was no fundamental difference between legal expropriation and *de facto* expropriation through inflation. The alienation of the German *Mittelstand* from their traditional political representatives in the DNVP exposed a dangerous political vacuum in German society. As the German Nationalists' share of the polls dropped

---

The Holzmans came to visit us. 'What Germany needs,' said father to Mr Holzman, 'is a sound and healthy middle class, and what the middle class needs is a strong middle class party.' Mr Holzman, a member of the Social Democratic Party said, 'It would be wiser for you to side with the workers against the monopolies.' Father replied, 'Good if only the workers would side with us instead of striking against us.'

The von Bülows ... also came to visit us, and father repeated, 'What Germany needs is a sound and healthy middle class and what the middle class needs is a strong middle class party.' To this, Mr von Bülow, a member of the German National Party, the party of the old reactionary group, replied, 'We have already more than enough parties as it is. Why don't you side with us. We shall see that law and order are restored at the port.' Father said, 'But who guarantees to us that you won't swallow us after we have checked the workers?'

(Pearl S. Buck, *How it Happens: talk about the German People 1914-1933 with Erna von Pustan*, New York 1947)

from its high point of six million in 1924 to little more than two million in 1932 a number of specifically 'middle-class parties' attempted to fill that vacuum. In 1926 a Party for People's Rights and Economic Revaluation was formed, in which the element of moral outrage at the manipulations of 'big business' was prominent. The decline of the 'old' middle class was lamented as the passing of an era of German greatness, and the 'silent socialisation' of small traders and producers through inflation was denounced as a trick of 'finance and monopoly capitalism'. In effect the party was little more than a safety valve for middle-class resentments, similar to the *Landvolk* movements which flourished in rural areas during the late 1920s. But the growth of such apparently bizarre political parties despite their lack of political influence strikingly illustrates the central dilemma of the German middle class during the Weimar era: namely, how could a social class, fragmented both socially and politically, join together to fight for the preservation of an archaic economic system – a system which was an anachronism both to proletarian socialism and to a modern form of capitalism characterised by trusts and high finance?

3

The Rise of Fascism

So how does man live?
When every hour he falls upon his fellow men,
Stripping, torturing, strangling and devouring.

The only way he can stay alive
Is by completely forgetting
that he is a human being!

(Bertolt Brecht)

The formation of the NSDAP

In the autumn of 1918, at about the time of the overthrow of the old Bavarian monarchy by the Independent Socialists under Kurt Eisner, a small society calling itself the Political Workers' Circle was formed in Munich. Led by the journalist Karl Harrer and a toolmaker from the city's railway workshop by the name of Anton Drexler, the Political Workers' Circle was a typical Bavarian *Stammtisch* group, meeting regularly in a local Beerhall to discuss politics. Despite the proletarian flavour of its title, the Political Workers' Circle was in fact a radical right-wing grouping with extreme anti-Semitic views. But until the overthrow of the Munich Workers' Republic in May 1919, the Circle, with an initial membership of seven persons, did little that might attract attention to its activities.

Anton Drexler, however, had great ambitions for the group which he led, and even during the first weeks of the Circle's existence he pushed for the setting up of a political party which could work in public for the group's aims. Thus on 5 January 1919, the Germany Workers' Party (DAP) was launched as the 'political' arm of the Political Workers' Circle.

The DAP remained a largely paper organisation until the summer of 1919. Then, in the climate of anti-socialist and anti-Semitic hysteria induced by the suppression of the Workers' Republic and the public trials of its leaders, the German Workers' Party gradually gained the confidence to expand its activities and even to stage public rallies. The party began to attract the interest of other Bavarian right-wing organisations, and before long it came to the attention of the Bavarian Reichswehr (army) who were ever on the look-out for suitable para-military organisations to swell their ranks secretly (the numbers of the German armed forces were at this time controlled by the Allies).

It was in his capacity as a propaganda officer in the Bavarian Reichswehr that Hitler came into contact with the DAP in August 1919, when he was ordered to report on its activities and potential. And although he was far from impressed by the organisation which he discovered, he was none the less encouraged by the 'good-will' which he found – presumably the vicious anti-Semitism which was Drexler's particular trait. Hitler joined the German Workers' Party in September 1919 and quickly rose to become the party's chief

Anton Drexler, co-founder of the German Workers'
Party (DAP).

nationalism. At about the same time the
party also changed its name to the
National Socialist German Workers' Party
(NSDAP) in line with Hitler's and
Drexler's intention to win over the working
class to some form of national corporatism.

In December 1920, Dietrich Eckart (who
was to become a close friend and confidant
of Hitler) purchased the independent
newspaper the *Völkischer Beobachter* for
the NSDAP with financial help from the
Bavarian Reichswehr. Since the party
newspaper was under the direct control of
the propaganda leader, the acquisition of
the *Völkischer Beobachter* presented
Hitler with a useful means of undermining
the 'old guard' around Drexler as well as

Two examples of the propaganda produced by the
early NSDAP. The leaflet (*opposite*), entitled 'A
Political Awakening', is entirely the work of Anton
Drexler and gives some idea of the role of anti-
Semitism at this stage in the party's development.
The cartoon (*below*) shows a German Jew inviting
Death to leave the ruins of Soviet Russia and enter
Germany: 'Enter Death. Our people in Germany have
made everything ready.'

progaganda officer and a member of the
Executive Committee largely because of
his obvious talent as a public speaker.
Indeed Hitler's ambition was matched only
by his impatience with the pseudo-
democratic structure of the DAP, which he
consistently referred to as a 'tea-club'
rather than a political party. But his initial
attempts to persuade the party membership to introduce an authoritarian organisational structure met with little success,
since they were opposed by Drexler and his
friends on the Executive Committee.
Unable to sway Drexler or his clique, Hitler
redoubled his attempts to attract new
members, hoping thereby to dilute the
influence of the 'old guard' and to increase
his personal power base.

As a first step Hitler drafted and published the so-called Twenty-five Point
Party Programme early in 1920 – a curious
mixture of anti-capitalism, anti-socialism,
anti-Semitism, corporatism and ultra-

National Socialist German Workers Party

A Political Awakening

Dear Colleagues,

It is a workmate who is speaking to you – one who still stands at the lathe.

What he has to say to you might seem rather strange and surprising; since it sounds very different to what you are accustomed to hear. ... I am a socialist like yourselves, and want manual workers to gain equality with all other creative groups, as well as the annihilation of layabouts and drones and the confiscation of profits earned without work or effort.

I still hope for a true and just form of socialism, the salvation of the working masses, and the freeing of creative mankind from the chains of exploitative capitalism.

But I am convinced that we are not on the right path to reach this goal ...

Many of our leaders are indeed honest men, and want the best for the workers. But there are also a number who are in the service of a foreign power.

They have used the workers' movement as an instrument for certain special interests; they have used the workers' organisations as a bodyguard for unproductive Stock Exchange and loan capitalism. As a result of my investigations, I am convinced:

There is a secret world conspiracy, which while speaking much about humanity and tolerence, in reality wants only to harness the people to a new yoke.

A number of workers' leaders belong to this group. The leaders are big capitalists ...

300 big bankers, financiers and press barons, who are interconnected across the world, are the real dictators. They belong almost exclusively to the 'chosen people'. They are all members of this same secret conspiracy, which organises world politics – namely the international Freemasons Lodge ... Their aim is:

THE DICTATORSHIP OF MONEY OVER WORK.

... These Bank and Stock Exchange dictators do nothing openly, for they have their agents in the workers' movement, and they pay them well. They turn people's resentment against them on to the small property owners, the factory owners and the farmers, who with all their money could hardly pay the interest owing to the big bankers. The House of Rothschild alone owns more capital than the whole of German heavy industry together ...

When will we finally see through the false friends of our movement? The Jewish big capitalist always plays our friend and dogooder; but he only does it to make us into his slaves. The trusting worker is going to help him to set up the world dictatorship of Jewry. Because that is their goal, as it states in the Bible. 'All the peoples will serve you, all the wealth of the world will belong to you' ... In the Talmud it says, 'a time is coming when every Jew will have 2800 slaves'.

Comrades, do you want to be Jewish slaves?

... An end to false pride! We workers always give it out that we have created all human culture with our bare hands. But is that right? ... What about teachers, inventors, artists, researchers and technicians?

Are the middle classes, the bourgeoisie and the farmers not productive? ... and don't they also suffer under the dictatorship of big capital, just like us? Wouldn't it make more sense to offer them our hand and together turn on our common enemy? ... It is the particular trick of the capitalist exploiters that they are able to play the workers and the bourgeoisie off one against the other, and thereby keep them powerless

...

Shake off your Jewish leaders, and those in the pay of Judas! ... And one final point. Don't expect anything from Bolshevism. It doesn't bring the worker freedom ... In Russia the eight-hour day has been abolished. There are no more workers' councils. All cower under the dictatorship of a hundred government commissars, who are nine-tenths Jewish.

Bolshevism is a Jewish swindle.

Anton Drexler, toolmaker.
Munich
1920

the opportunity to propagate his own views and beliefs among the party membership. Additionally, as the party continued to expand its influence, a central party newspaper gave Hitler direct access to the influx of provisional members. Control of the *Völkischer Beobachter*, with a circulation of 10,000 – 15,000 during 1921, was therefore a second major step in Hitler's strategy for seizing control of the NSDAP.

The first local organisation outside Munich was formed at Rosenheim in April 1920, and by early 1921 the NSDAP had a dozen branches outside the Bavarian capital. The First National Congress of the NSDAP was held on 22 January 1921, when the membership stood at approximately 3,000. Yet despite its name as a National Socialist Workers' movement the rank and file of the NSDAP was made up almost exclusively of members of the German *Mittelstand*, with very few proletarian recruits. More important, the recent increase in membership was very much due to the efforts of Hitler and his 'circle': men such as Alfred Rosenberg, Hermann Esser and Dietrich Eckart. At the congress there was much criticism of Hitler's 'bohemian life-style' from the old leadership, and comments about the unsavoury character of many of his immediate associates. But while Hitler's presence at the salon parties of Bavarian high society was felt to detract from the NSDAP's image as a populist movement, the generous financial contributions to the fledgeling party from the Bechstein family and others of Munich's wealthy elite were never refused.

In July 1921 the executive of the NSDAP (which as a result of a technical change no longer included Hitler) made an agreement with the German Socialist Party to merge their branches in Augsburg as a first step in creating a single unified organisation, whose national leadership would be based in Berlin. There can be little doubt that Drexler and his friends wanted to counter Hitler's strong personal following in Bavaria by this move. Hitler's reaction was swift. He resigned from the party. The executive responded by publishing a leaflet warning that Hitler wished to assume dictatorial control of the NSDAP and criticising once more his bohemian habits; but they added the manifestly absurd charge that Hitler was a Jewish agent and a secret supporter of the monarchy.

Two days after his 'resignation' Hitler issued a letter setting out his preconditions for rejoining the party. He basically demanded to be elected chairman of the NSDAP with dictatorial powers, and he called for the convening of a special conference to put the issue to the vote. In the face of his intransigence Drexler's clique was powerless, for even if they could operate without the powerful attraction of Hitler's personality the party could hardly prosper without his well-connected and well-heeled crowd of admirers. Drexler reluctantly opted to accept Hitler's

ultimatum rather than see the party collapse, and the rest of the executive could not hope to carry the membership without Drexler's support. At the special congress held on 29 January the old board resigned their offices and Hitler was elected first chairman by 553 votes to one. The new leader appointed his supporters to the major positions of influence within the party, although he shrewdly retained Drexler as head of a 'Reconciliation Committee' to smooth out possible difficulties outside his Munich power-base. Eckart became editor of the *Völkischer Beobachter*, Esser took control of propaganda, and Hitler himself headed the Investigation Committee, since this could be used to purge unco-operative party members and was therefore a means of furthering his authority.

In moving to consolidate his position, Hitler appointed his former army sergeant Max Amman to the post of business manager of the NSDAP. Amman was not even in the party at the time, but his qualities of personal integrity and managerial competence were recognised by a wide cross-section of the provincial party branches. In effect Amman was a 'Hitlerman', but since he was not identified with any of the warring factions his reorganisation of the party's administration gained general acceptance. By November 1921 the NSDAP had some 13 full-time officials with an efficient centralised bureaucracy; and early in 1922 Hitler was able to extend his authority to allow him to expel entire party branches, not merely individual members. The National Socialist Party thus became a rigidly authoritarian political organisation in which local branches were forbidden to undertake any form of joint activity with other political organisations without Hitler's express permission. Even the production of propaganda material was centrally controlled. Nearly all party posters and leaflets were issued in Munich, and any local material had first to be approved by party headquarters.

Colleagues   Beware!   Comrades

THE ANTI-SEMITES WANT TO INCITE YOU

Workers, Bürger, Soldiers, Women!

SUPPORT US!
for:

Who are the big capitalists à la Rothschild, Bleichröder, Schwabach?	We Jews!
Who has a greater annual income than Krupp's fortune?	A Jew!
Who made the revolution, paid for it, and now wants the rewards?	We Jews!
Who led and paid the Spartacists and the Bolsheviks?	We Jews!
Who alone is 'international', yet is a united race amongst a divided and incited people?	We Jews!
Who offers you truly licentious art in the cinema, cabaret and theatre, and wants Christian morality to go to the Devil?	We Jews!
Who sees to it that you can buy on the black market all those goods which are supposed to be 'unavailable'?	We Jews!
Who destroys all bonds of honour, family, nation and society?	We Jews!
Who frees you from large families, just so that our own brood can develop nicely?	We Jews!
Who pushes taxes high, so that the banks need not go short?	We Jews!

Who frees you from ridiculous German honour, art and customs?
Who roots out both protestantism and catholicism?
Who protects instead
his own Mosaic religion and secret Talmud teachings?

WE JEWS!

So join one of our Jewish controlled political parties.
We Jews Are Your Masters!

We will soon suppress the couple of Germans who want to protect you –
the swastika-louts and the *völkisch* rabble-rousers.
We'll suppress them just like you.
We'll do it again with your help, dear workers!
Workers You must be proud to be our slaves and our servants!
We'll pay for everything. You needn't do anything else,
We'll feed you for the rest of your life.

So workers, be our bodyguards! True until death! We have had to withdraw
all our capital for your benefit, so that we are now quite poor.

Help Us Dear Worker! Cause a riot in every opponent's meeting! Rip any
leaflet up, unread, that tries to open your eyes. You May Not Read It!

Make the Nazis despicable, by calling them Anti-Semitic
Rowdies, then the German bourgeoisie will fall into line.

A member of the Jewish race.

Printed Munich.

Nazi leaflet, 1922

Hitler attends 'German Day' in Hof (northern Bavaria) on 16 September 1923. Ten days later he took over command of the Bavarian *Kampfbund*.

The Munich Beerhall coup

Early in 1923 the crisis in the occupied Rhineland and the much-rumoured insurrectionary intentions of the Communists in Saxony and Thuringia convinced Hitler that his best chance of gaining political power lay in allying himself and the party with the plans of the Bavarian right for a 'March on Berlin'. The authoritarian Bavarian government under Ritter von Kahr (who had seized power illegally during the Kapp putsch) was very much associated with these plans, as was the Bavarian Reichswehr, which expected to enrol the support of army groups in central and northern Germany to set up a national military dictatorship. Certainly, while the pretext of suppressing a Communist insurrection in central Germany remained, an armed putsch was a viable political option, and Hitler prepared the National Socialists to play a leading role. Gradually then, the para-military wing of the NSDAP, known as the

Stormtroopers, or SA, began to over-shadow the political arm of the party, as the emphasis shifted from political organisation and propaganda activity towards military preparations for a coup (the SA or *Sturmabteilung* was formed in July 1921 ostensibly to protect party meetings from attack by political opponents).

The NSDAP Congress in 1923 very much demonstrated this change in strategy. There was no discussion of party policy. Instead, Hitler announced the official line and the assembled party members applauded. In place of political debate was military spectacle. Hitler reviewed a parade of the party's Stormtroopers designed to emphasise their martial discipline and military capability, rounding off the proceedings with a solemn dedication of the party's flags and standards. Consultations with the

67

commander-in-chief of the Reichswehr and with right-wing industrialists, headed by Hugo Stinnes, followed; and when Hitler was appointed political leader of the *Kampfbund* – a confederation of Bavarian Freecorps and paramilitary units – it seemed as if he was on the threshold of political success. But his expectancy was premature.

The overthrow of the left-wing governments in Saxony and Thuringia late in the summer of 1923 not only removed the pretext for armed intervention, it also left the illegal von Kahr regime politically exposed. The national government under Stresemann, having suppressed legal leftist rule in central Germany, was now under pressure to act against the far-right in Bavaria, who were in flagrant breach of the constitution. Besides, the allies were making threatening noises about the existence of a large military formation in Bavaria, and the Reichswehr High Command, despite its sympathy with the political aims of the Bavarian armed forces, warned against any attempt at a putsch. In the hope of reaching some form of political accommodation, the von Kahr regime put out discreet feelers to Stresemann, who proved only too willing to respond, given his doubts about the feasibility of ordering the Reichswehr to disarm right-wing nationalists.

On 6 November von Kahr informed the *Kampfbund* that a March on Berlin was no longer possible, and that the Bavarian army would have no choice but to intervene against any attempt to stage a coup. Hitler was furious. He had sacrificed his political independence and staked all on the willingness of the armed forces to support the putsch attempt. Von Kahr's decision condemned him to the political wilderness, and Hitler had no intention of accepting such a verdict. He made immediate preparations to by-pass the ministers and generals by carrying out a coup at the head of his own Stormtroops. Once an insurrection was underway, Hitler believed that the military would also fall into line, even without the support of its high-ranking officers.

National Socialist Stormtroopers parade near Munich in 1922.

Troops taking part in the Hitler-coup gather outside the Bürgerbräukeller on 9 November 1923.

On the evening of 8 November von Kahr was scheduled to speak at the Bürgerbräukeller, together with a number of his ministers. Under cover of darkness SA units surrounded the Beerhall, and in best theatrical tradition Adolf Hitler strode up to the speaker's rostrum, fired a pistol shot into the ceiling and announced: 'The national revolution has begun!' While the three-thousand-strong audience looked on bemused, Hitler alternately threatened and pleaded with von Kahr to give his sanction to a March on Berlin. In the meantime he sent for General Ludendorff and offered him military command of the *coup d'état* in recognition of Ludendorff's status as 'Germany's greatest war-hero'. Eventually von Kahr gave his consent, and an overjoyed Hitler left the hall to prevent a confrontation between his Stormtroopers and a local Reichswehr regiment. Inside the Beerhall there was an atmosphere of excitement and high optimism among the Nazi Stormtroopers, for the gamble appeared to have paid off; and when von Kahr and his ministers slipped out of the building in the early hours of the morning nobody apparently noticed.

When dawn broke on 9 November the situation had changed dramatically. Hitler found himself isolated in the eastern suburbs of Munich with the police force and Reichswehr units deployed against him in the city's government quarters. Initially inclined to seek some form of political amnesty for himself and his followers, Hitler let himself be persuaded by Ludendorff that all was not lost. Ludendorff proposed to march at the head of a column which would advance to the city centre, believing that his charisma alone would prevent the police from opening fire. Thus the troop of some three thousand National Socialists and supporters set off with Hitler and Ludendorff in the lead, crossed the River Isar and headed towards the Feldherrnhalle (Soldiers' Hall) – the greatest symbol of German military might in Munich. As the column approached the Feldherrnhalle, Hitler and Ludendorff found the way blocked by a cordon of armed police. For a few seconds the column halted, but Ludendorff strode forward and the front ranks followed. The police opened fire! Shooting lasted less than a minute before the National Socialists scattered and fled, leaving fourteen dead and many wounded. Hitler's arm was dislocated as he dived for cover, and he was rapidly spirited away from the scene by car. Hermann

69

Many high-ranking civil servants were also deeply implicated in the coup. Pöhner, the Police President of Munich, sided with the putschists and took part in the coup.

Göring, an early member of the NSDAP, was shot in the thigh and carried into a nearby bank where he received first-aid from the Jewish manager. A few hours later, Hitler was arrested and charged with treason – a crime which carried the death penalty.

Hitler's trial and imprisonment

The collapse of the putsch, Hitler's arrest and imprisonment and the banning of the NSDAP were virtually simultaneous developments. The party organisation had been neglected in favour of strengthening the SA, so that there was no long term political strategy to fall back upon, and certainly no preparations had been made for the NSDAP to lead an underground existence.

The National Socialists rapidly disintegrated into a chaos of warring factions, with each faction claiming to uphold the 'true values of the Hitler movement'. Those activisits who attempted to maintain the cohesion of the old party under some form of cover organisation were also unsuccessful, with groups such as the Patriotic Alpine Club and the Bavarian Flora and Fauna Society being disbanded by the police for beginning their proceedings with Nazi songs and carrying the swastika flag on 'field-trips'. In effect Hitler had been the one person capable of holding the NSDAP together despite deep-seated differences within the party over political doctrine and tactics, so that without his leadership the movement fell apart.

In prison Hitler refused to mediate or lend his personal authority to any particular faction – which only served to strengthen his image as the National Socialist Movement's 'natural' leader and encourage further bickering and disunity among his supporters. These conflicts reflected both regional and ideological differences. In northern areas of Germany, where Hitler had never been able to extend his personal influence as fully as in Bavaria, groups who identified with National Socialism tended to be made up of younger, more radical activists. They were highly sceptical of the 'old-timers' in Munich and regarded many of the party leaders as reactionaries who were attempting to restore some type of pre-war authoritarian system. Squabbles over ideology were also deep-rooted. Many northern branches still favoured some form of alliance between revolutionary working-class socialism and *petit bourgeois* nationalism. On the other hand, the lure of anti-Semitism was particularly strong in Bavaria, and nowhere more so than in Nuremberg, where Julius Streicher led a group of National Socialists dedicated to 'eliminating' Jewish influence in the city.

3. The Rise of Fascism

Even the failure of the coup had done little to diminish the faith of many Nazis in the possibility of overthrowing the hated Weimar system by force, and this continued emphasis upon military conspiracy meant that activists were trapped in a mire of ultra-right-wing rivalry and leadership disputes.

The far right was however able to capitalise on the excitement generated by Hitler's attempted *coup d'état*. At elections held early in 1924 an alliance of racist organisations known as the *Völkischer* Block gained half a million votes, becoming the third largest party in the Bavarian parliament. Hitler's trial was unfortunately timed to begin during the final run-up to the election, and its impact was largely responsible for the *Völkischer* Block's success. The court-room drama unfolded in a circus-like atmosphere of good will between the prosecution and the defence, and Hitler seized the opportunity to enhance his personal reputation and to launch an attack upon his political enemies. 'I have resolved to be the destroyer of Marxism,' he proclaimed. 'We wanted to create order in the state, throw out the drones and take up the fight against Stock Exchange slavery.' His propaganda task was made easier by the efforts of the prosecution to exonerate Ludendorff, whose prestige made him an unwelcome defendant in the dock. Indeed Hitler was only too happy to be identified as the real driving force behind the coup. In his final defence speech Hitler launched into a remarkable diatribe against the conservative establishment for their 'cowardice', insisting that he alone had the necessary courage and will to lead the struggle against the 'Jewish republic'. In the final act of the sham proceedings Hitler was sentenced to five years' 'honourable confinement' with the understanding that

The accused in the 'Hitler-trial' pose outside the courtroom.

PERNET WEBER FRICK KRIEBEL LUDENDORFF HITLER BRÜCKNER RÖHM WAGNER

he would be released on probation after twelve months.

During his comfortable confinement in Landsberg Castle Hitler dictated the first part of his autobiography *Mein Kampf* ('My Struggle') and thought about how he could rebuild the party upon his release. The failure of the putsch convinced him that any further attempt to overthrow the republic by force would be futile, especially as politically conditions were tending to stabilise after 1923 with the ending of hyper-inflation. Besides, a *coup d'état* needed the support of the army, and his experience in November left him with an ingrained distrust of the military hierarchy. Therefore the NSDAP of the pre-putsch era, effectively a para-military elite manoeuvering in a twilight world of double-dealing and conspiracy, would have to be restructured to take into account the demands of modern political life. The movement needed to build a mass following which was not confined to southern Germany and with a broad appeal to all social classes. To this end even participation in local and national elections might be an expedient method of gaining political power. Shortly after the unexpected success of the *Völkischer* Block in the 1924 elections Hitler is recorded as saying: 'We shall have to hold our noses and enter the Reichstag against the Catholic and Marxist deputies.' (Kurt Ludecke, *I Knew Hitler*, London 1938, p. 217).

Rebuilding the party

Although Hitler well understood the need to expand the influence of National Socialism outside Bavaria and southern Germany, he realised also that the process of creating a national movement would have to begin in Munich, where his personal following and indeed the cult of the Führer was strongest. Upon his release from prison in December 1924 Hitler maintained his public silence, refusing to make any pronouncements or identify with

'First Bread then Reparations'. A typical NSDAP propaganda poster of the time, showing 'the Jew' together with the Versailles Treaty and the Dawes Plan as responsible for Germany's plight. The Dawes Plan of 1924 allowed German reparation payments to 'return to Germany' in the form of loans – initially some 800 million gold marks. In return the allies demanded the denationalisation of the German railways, designed to bring in 660 million marks in interest payments.

Same line by KPD

any of the remaining party factions until the lifting of the ban on the NSDAP in Bavaria.

Hitler's first major speech was cleverly scheduled to take place at the Bürgerbräukeller on 27 February 1925. Amid a frenzy of excitement and expectation he delivered a masterly monologue designed to rally all factions of the party around his leadership. He reaffirmed his beliefs in the 'inviolable principles of National Socialism' – against Marxism and the Jews – and once again demanded dictatorial powers over the party membership. By late March, he had accepted oaths of personal loyalty from nearly all Bavarian party branches, after which he set out to establish his absolute authority and 'create order' among National Socialists in the rest of Germany.

In northern Germany, however, those groups sympathetic to National Socialism were not so easily subjugated to the absolutism of the 'Führer-principle'. They owed little to Hitler's magnetic style of leadership and were concentrated in the larger towns and industrial conurbations, where the membership consisted mainly of

the uprooted *petite bourgeoisie*, many of whom had seen service in the Freecorps. Despite their hostility to Marxism, they maintained a healthy respect for the fighting qualities of the revolutionary workers, and even flirted with some form of 'national-Bolshevism'. So when Hitler deliberately isolated the National Socialists from the rest of the ultra-right by endorsing General Ludendorff as the party's candidate for the 1925 presidential elections, instead of accepting Karl Jarres

Election leaflet from Baden, 25 October 1925. The content is clearly designed to appeal to left-wing working class voters, but note the 'electoral alliance' with the middle-class Revaluation movement.

German Workers!

The November revolution, the revolution of the Jews and the Marxist party-rabble have delivered you into the hands of international loan capitalism. For years you have sweated so that the State can pay the interest on its loan capital. You are damned for all eternity to be wage-slaves, if you don't demand:

1. The Nationalisation of the banks and the money economy.
2. The abolition of interest-exploiters and Stock Exchange speculators.
3. The abolition of mobile (share) capital.

Vote

on October 25th for
Nat. Soc. German Worker
(Hitler) Party, Völkisch and
Revaluation movement.

IS THIS YOUR STRUGGLE AGAINST CAPITALISM, MARXIST?

The National Socialists have introduced into the Reichstag the following resolution, relating to a law for

THE EXPROPRIATION OF THE FORTUNE OF THE BANK AND STOCK EXCHANGE PRINCES AND OTHER PARASITES.

Article 1.

The total fortune of bank and Stock Exchange princes, the eastern Jews who since August 1914 have moved in, and other foreign elements, together with their families and family hangers-on, further the profits of war, revolution, inflation and deflation, will be expropriated without compensation for the well-being of the community.

The expropriated fortunes will belong to the states in which the owners live or are to be found.

Article 2.

The expropriated fortunes will be used to benefit:
a)   the unemployed
b)   war invalids and war-widows
c)   old age pensioners
d)   the victims of inflation
e)   farm labourers, peasants and subsistence farmers, who will settle the expropriated land.

By refusing this Resolution the bourgeois parties, but above all the Marxist parties, have shown themselves clearly to be

CAPITALIST SLAVES

and that they don't give a damn about the plight of honest creative people.

Racial Colleagues!

Our call goes out to you who earn your bread through honest work. If you don't want your children, and your children's children to be damned for all eternity as slaves of world capitalism, if you don't want to be made into the protectors of Stock Exchange bandits and other blood suckers by your treacherous leaders, if you are on the contrary filled with a fanatical will for freedom, then join the ranks of

National Socialist German Workers Party

Printed Munich. Content responsibility of Gregor Strasser. 1926.

das Dein Kampf gegen
Kapitalismus, Marxist?

malsozialisten brachten im Reichstage folgenden Antrag ein auf ein Gesetz über

teignung des Vermögens der Bank- und
rsenfürsten u. anderer Volksparasiten.

The 'capitalist Jew' sitting on his bag of loot (*above*) (the profits of 'war, revolution and inflation') is protected from the Nazi 'worker' by a Marxist street-fighter. The leaflet (*left*) illustrates the NSDAP's attempts to exploit anti-capitalist sentiment without at the same time supporting genuine socialism. Thus the 'parasitic' elements of capitalism are identified with the Jews, allowing the party to support simultaneously private property and the principles of the free market economy.

shift the balance of the party's ideology towards a more populist course, convinced that the 'reactionaries' in Munich were influencing Hitler's judgment. But attempts to pursue a 'radical' strategy had organisational and ideological consequences, as Hitler well understood.

A 'radical' strategy involved the NSDAP in attempting to set up some form of racist trade union in order to challenge the power of the socialists and Communists in the labour movement. Hitler was particularly hostile to such a course of action, for it would ultimately challenge the authoritarian principles of the party and hence his own absolute leadership. Ideologically, too, the 'radical' strategy was suspect. Class struggle was deemed to be more important than racial struggle, and since insufficient qualification could be made between what was called 'Jewish' or 'parasitic', capitalism and 'German' or 'creative' capitalism, Hitler feared that the party would be identified as anti-capitalist and hence lose the support of the propertied classes. Even so, Hitler deliberately avoided bringing matters to a head throughout 1925, and gave both sides hints that he was personally in favour of their particular viewpoints. But the crisis could not be ignored indefinitely, as support for the party was ebbing away.

On 4 February 1926 Hitler acted decisively and with cunning. He invited the leaders of the northern districts, among them Gregor Strasser and Joseph Goebbels, to a secret conference at Bamberg in northern Bavaria, ostensibly to discuss the party's differences. In fact Hitler packed the meeting with members sympathetic to reactionary proposals and entirely loyal to his leadership. Moreover he chose Bamberg as a town particularly strong in its support for the NSDAP in order to impress upon the opposition the paltry strength of their own backing in the north, where branches were fortunate if they could summon a dozen members to a local meeting. After a 'debate' lasting five hours, in which Hitler was the only speaker

as a compromise choice, relations between the two wings of the party reached crisis point. (By endorsing Ludendorff in a hopeless campaign, Hitler ensured the General's political humiliation and thereby strengthened his own claim to leadership of the far-right in Bavaria.) Many northern members left the party in disillusionment at what they saw as Hitler's ambiguous and vacillating leadership and joined rival *völkisch* organisations. Those who remained fought to

and in which he opposed almost all the 'radical' proposals, Hitler challenged the thoroughly intimidated minority to 'trample upon the holy memory of the National Socialist dead' and deny his own 'divinely ordained leadership'. Not surprisingly, they chose to submit. Shortly afterwards, Goebbels was invited to Munich as 'the personal guest of the Führer' and granted the honour of a long audience with Hitler. Goebbels was overwhelmed. After the meeting he wrote in his diary: 'Hitler is a great man. He forgives us and he shakes our hand. Let us forget the past.' Only a few days earlier he had written, 'Hitler is a reactionary!'

Goebbels' conversion was a milestone in the history of the party. Although the NSDAP had been unable to make any real impact upon the national political scene since Hitler's release from prison, the carefully cultured image of dynamism and party unity which could be presented after Bamberg began to draw admiring glances from other right-wing associations. At the Weimar Congress in 1926 a number of *völkisch* groups were sufficiently impressed by the fervent atmosphere of 'will and fanaticism' to propose total merger with the National Socialists. But the problem remained of translating this success into effective political agitation outside the confines of the German extreme right.

At the time of the Weimar Congress the membership of the NSDAP numbered some 35,000, and although not large by the standards of the major German political parties, the NSDAP was characterised by the high percentage of militants in its ranks (over 10 per cent of the membership attended the Weimar Congress). On the other hand political conditions no longer looked favourably upon a party which fed upon the various resentments of the middle classes. During the mid-1920s the German economy gradually stabilised, and largely as a result of an influx of American loans a period of comparative economic growth occurred. Real wages were increasing, unemployment was decreasing and with

the election of the war-General Paul von Hindenburg to the Presidency in April 1925, the republic even seemed assured of a certain legitimacy in the eyes of the *bourgeoisie*.

In fact the carefully cultured image of power and unity projected at the Weimar Congress papered over the very real ambiguity of Hitler's political strategy in 1926. While accepting that elections could be a useful method of generating support for the National Socialist movement, Hitler was still not convinced of the need totally to identify the party with the democratic process. Not until November 1927 did he accept that an electoral strategy could have a real chance of success, and in the meantime there were considerable sections within the party who made their opposition to electoral participation noisily apparent. There is no doubt that Hitler still hoped to emulate the Italian fascists' 'March on Rome', although he rejected the option of a military putsch which had failed so dismally in 1923. But the Italian facists had not relied upon armed might alone; rather they had built up mass support and an effective political organisation which had paralysed the major centres of economic life in Italy. That a similar scenario was conceived by the NSDAP leadership in 1926 is suggested by a speech in which Goebbels talked of making 'two dozen cities into the unshakable foundations of our movement'. If the NSDAP could win power in the factories and on the streets, then Hitler believed he could still emulate the career of his great hero Benito Mussolini.

Into the cities!

In October 1926 Joseph Goebbels was appointed leader of the NSDAP's Berlin organisation in an attempt to bring the unruly membership under control, as well as to initiate the first phase of a strategy of consolidating support for the party in key areas. The Berlin organisation was notoriously radical and strongly *anti-*

The SA at Frankfurt am Main.

bourgeois: as the leader of the propaganda section in Neukölln stated, 'We are sick to the teeth with all sections of the middle classes'. Yet despite some local successes in Berlin, as well as in Hamburg and the Ruhr, the National Socialists were unable to compete effectively with either the SPD or the KPD, nor could they win the support of any significant section of the working class. The party still had no alternative union structure to offer. But most important, the Nazi Stormtroopers could not hope to match the street fighters of the Communit Red Front in the proletarian quarters of industrial cities. An attempt towards the end of 1926 to strengthen the fighting capability of the SA by forming a common front with two other right-wing para-military associations (the *Stahlhelm* and the *Wehrwolf*) came to nothing, and in view of this failure Hitler had no alternative but to revitalise the spirit of his own Stormtroopers by thoroughly reorganising the SA's role within the party.

Hitler was still fearful of the Stormtroopers as a potentially independent force who might jeopardise the whole movement by a second putsch attempt. Yet he also realised that 'we have to teach Marxism that National Socialism is master of the streets, just as one day it will

be master of the state'. Therefore, he announced, 'the training of the SA must be undertaken in accordance with the needs of the party, not according to military criteria ... (the SA) must not be secretive, but should march in the open ... we don't need daring conspirators, but one hundred thousand fighters for our cause' (letter from Hitler to von Pfeffer, head of the SA).

In November 1926 Franz von Pfeffer was nominated to take charge of the new SA in the hope that he could curtail the Stormtroopers' *penchant* for aimless street brawls and radical phraseology, and create instead a propaganda shock-troop for the National Socialist movement. Results, however, were slow in coming. The Munich SA rebelled against attempts to curtail their independence, and it took Hitler's personal intervention, and the assurance that he too would sooner be a 'simple SA man', rather than the movement's Führer, to bring them into line. Then in May 1927, after weeks of provocation and bloody street fights involving the Berlin SA, the Prussian police banned the whole of the NSDAP's Berlin organisation.

In effect the NSDAP had marched down a *cul de sac*. By concentrating scarce resources upon large urban centres and attempting to undermine the allegiance of the working class to their traditional socialist organisations (whether revolu-

"The German people have won all along the line"

lied the heroes of November 1918 …
cried the 'Frankfurter Zeitung', central organ of the

INTERNATIONAL FINANCE-HYENAS

The German people have had ten years to find out just how this victory looks in reality.

WHERE IS THE INTERNATIONAL WORLD REVOLUTION?

It's overdue! The revolution just managed to chisel off the royal insignia from the facade of the post-office, and then it was finished. The storm of the red batallions was spent. It cost a couple of broken windows and a few dead Volkscomrades.

That was the Revolution of the Social Democracy!

THE RED BOSSES
THE BLACK TOP-HATTERS
and THE GOLDEN DEMOCRATS

have together delivered our people, sold out and defenceless,

INTO THE HANDS OF INTERNATIONAL WORLD CAPITAL.

"The German army is invincible, but I trust in the German Social Democrats": so said the Englishman Loyd [sic] George.

I love the German Social Democrats because I wish

THE PEST ON GERMANY

So wrote the Frenchman Leon Daudet. Didn't they put their trust in the right place?

Haven't we seen the pest in Germany during the last ten years? Black Frenchmen and slimy Polacks in the service of international high finance, and because of the treason of the 9th November, they have become the slave-drivers of Germany.

The German worker lies in beauty and honour on the streets! ... Hunger, unemployment, misery, feebleness, tax-torture, inflation-swindles, corruption, bank-scandals, rubber-truncheons, smash and grab,

those are the results of the Revolution.

GERMANY IS WORTH LESS THAN A NIGGER STATE IN THE WORLD.

The eight-hour day you know only from the picture books of the Social Democrats. And whilst in the midst of our state, the "bourgeoisie" and the "proletariat" smash in each other's skulls, sinking together into the yoke of slavery,

THE INTERNATIONAL STOCK EXCHANGE JEWS TRIUMPH

over the bodies of the proletariat and the plundered Mittelstand.

Do you want it to go on forever? Then vote for Scheide- and Strese- men.

Then vote for the capitalist Dawes parties.

But if you want our race to free itself from today's conditions, then join up with the one party which has prophesied for the last eight years that it would come to this. Join up with the party which is the fanatical enemy of today's state, and which is hated most by its founders, from the Jewish newspaper of the world Stock Exchange, the Frankfurter Zeitung, to the Marxist paper famed for its lies, the Berliner Vorwärts.

VOTE FOR LIST 10

National Socialist German Workers Party (Hitler Movement).

---

tionary or reformist) the National Socialists had neglected their traditional source of support in the middle class. While the extreme right-wing character of the party never changed, there were just too many dissenting voices pleading for some form of classless society, and too many impoverished militants in the ranks of the SA who believed that Hitler really did want 'socialism' as well as 'nationalism'. The old core of the movement began to drift away. Falling membership meant a drop in revenue and, when Hitler met businessmen to plead for financial support for his party's struggle against Marxism, he was told in no uncertain terms that the radical rhetoric of the party's 'left-wing' was too much to stomach.

A case study: the farmers of Schleswig Holstein

In 1927 the farming community in Schleswig Holstein was set in ferment by a chronic agricultural recession. A series of poor harvests and low market prices combined with the outbreak of foot-and-mouth disease to threaten many thousands of farmers with ruin. Indeed the social effects

* What was revol. about the KPD?

Above Goebbels heads the march-in of the SA into the
Kriegervereinhaus, Wedding, Berlin, 1928.

of the crisis were exaggerated as small
farmers were unable to obtain credit to
cover their short-term debts because the
hyper-inflation had annihilated most rural
banks and credit agencies. Those most
seriously in debt mortgaged their farms
and land to large commercial banks, and
when in turn this credit was eaten up,
farmers and their families were faced with
eviction and destitution.

Initially the peasant proprietors turned
to their traditional political representatives for rescue – the German Nationalist
Party (DNVP) and the Farmers' League.
However, as the urban *petite bourgeoisie*
had learned to their cost in 1923, the
DNVP was the party of big business and it
was the free trade policy demanded by
heavy industry which had been largely
responsible for the crisis in agriculture in
the first place. (A free trade policy was
essential for the profitability of German
industry since exports accounted for such a
large percentage of turnover in a country
still suffering from the long-term economic
effects of a lost war, hyper-inflation and
the need to pay reparations. But a free

trade policy also meant that agricultural
imports, especially from Poland and
Denmark, were able to flood the German
market and drive down agricultural prices
when poor harvests at home would
normally have raised prices and maintained farmers' incomes.) Conversely, local
populist movements such as the *Landvolk*,
although demanding radical measures to
deal with the crisis, could not exert
political influence on a national level. In
effect, the Landvolk movement, despite
bombing campaigns against local tax
offices and violent demonstrations against
the expropriation of property belonging to
farmers, simply encouraged radicalism
without having the means to satisfy radical
demands.

It was the National Socialists, armed
with policies and propaganda specifically
designed to appeal to the small producer
and the 'little man', who were able to
exploit this reservoir of bitterness and pent
up frustration. In particular the Nazis'
prophecies of doom and destruction; their
offer of utopian solutions to complex
economic problems; their ability to speak

Above Peasant farmers at meal-time.

Below Schleswig-Holstein farmers take part in a demonstration to prevent compulsory eviction of a peasant farmer, 1928.

Farmers blockade the entrance to a farm to prevent the eviction of the farmer and his family, while local police look on.

'The Last Cow, or the outcome of Young politics!'

'Whoever decries National Socialism takes away the last hope from the farmer
'The farmer cannot live alone, if the German people should die
'Only one person can save the German people: HITLER and his brown army.'

Nazi leaflet from 1929 linking the acceptance of the Young Plan (to regulate reparations) with the increasing number of defaulting farmers. Note the figure of the 'Jew' overseeing the seizure of the 'last cow'.

GERMAN FARMERS!

Farmers, it is a matter of your house and home!

We told you years ago but you didn't listen, just like the rest of the German people. The middle classes should have listened during the years of the insane inflation. Now they have been annihilated: their possessions and savings have been stolen — expropriated!

The German worker expected the revolution to bring honour and beauty into his life. Now he is (to the extent that he can find work) the starving wage-slave of the Bank-Jews.

AND NOW IT'S YOUR TURN GERMAN FARMERS!

Factories, forests, railways, taxes and the state's finances have all been robbed by the Jew. Now he's stretching his greedy fingers towards the last German possession — the German countryside.

You farmer, will be chased from your plot of earth, which you have inherited from your forefathers since time immemorial.

Insatiable Jewish race-lust and fanaticism are the driving forces behind this devilish attempt to break Germany's backbone through the annihilation of the German farming community.

Wake up! Listen to something other than the daily twaddle printed in your local rags, which have hidden the truth from you for years.

Doesn't it open your eyes when you see the economy of the countryside being crippled by unnaturally high taxes, while you have no commensurate income to set off against this because of low prices for livestock and grain?

Don't you see the vile plan?! The same Jews who control **the monopoly on sales of nitrogen, calcium and phosphorus**, thereby dictating to you the high price of essential fertilizers, never give you a just price for your produce on the *Stock Exchange*.

Huge imports of frozen meat and foreign grain, at lowest prices, undercut you and push down your earnings.

The protective tariffs which the state has imposed are insufficient — not to say worthless. That same state is totally Jew-ridden in all its organs, and today can be called Germany in name only.

Nevertheless the prices of groceries are rising sharply in the towns day by day, driving your hungry German brothers to despair. Under the eyes of the so-called authorities the Jew is running a lucrative **middle-man Stock Exchange**.

And one thing more which is ruining you. You cannot obtain credit to tide you over these hard times. If you want money the usurous interest rates will wring your neck. Under the protection of the state it won't be long before the greater part of the land-owning farmers will be driven from their farms and homes by Jewish money lenders.

The plight of the German farmer is desperate.

Think it all over in your last few hours, and remember — we have been telling you the same thing for years!

Once again we're coming to you. This time you won't laugh at us!

BUT IT'S NEVER TOO LATE!

A people that has the will to live and struggle will survive.

Don't stand on the sidelines. Join our struggle against the Jews and loan capital!

Help us build a new Germany that will be

NATIONALIST AND SOCIALIST

Nationalist because it is free and held in respect.

Socialist because any German who works and creates, will be guaranteed not just a slave's ration of bread, but an honourable life, decent earnings and the sanctity of his hard-earned property.

Farmers, it is a matter of the most holy possession of a people,

THE LAND AND THE FIELDS
WHICH GOD HAS GIVEN US

Farmers, it is a matter of house and home,
Of life and death,
Of our people and our fatherland!

THEREFORE FARMER — WAKE UP!

Join the ranks of our defence force.   Fight with us

in the NATIONAL SOCIALIST GERMAN WORKERS PARTY

Munich 1927

---

the 'language' of the small farming communities; and their exploitation of traditional anti-Semitism, proved irresistable to many rural audiences.

A new way forward

By the beginning of 1928 there were clear signs that the Munich leadership was seeking new political pastures. Much to the surprise of party leaders, the NSDAP made some impressive gains in the Reichstag elections (20 May 1928) in western Schleswig-Holstein, parts of Hannover and the rural areas of Upper Franconia and Nuremberg – gains which at least partly

Traders!
Small Producers! Artisans!

For a long time you have kept out of sight and let corruption, favouritism and the nepotism of others run all over you. You believed that obeying law and order was the first duty of the citizen.

But what has this led to? Ever more exploitation by those in power. The tax-screw being turned ever tighter. You are the helots of this system. Your only job is to work and pay taxes which go into the salaries and pensions of ministers.

What have your parties done for you? They promised the world but did nothing. They made coalitions, prattled away before the elections then disappeared into parliament until the next.

They didn't unite against the treacherous leaders of Marxism.

They horse-dealt over ministerial posts and never gave you a thought.

They have ruled with Social Democrats and forgotten the aim of that party – Death to the Middle Class!

Have you forgotten the inflation? How you were robbed of your savings and commercial capital?

Have you forgotten how taxes have slowly throttled your businesses?

Have you forgotten how the Department Stores and the Co-operatives have ruined you?

… Middle classes, why is it so bad? Why are your shops empty? Why are you out of business?

Look at the banks and their massive profits! They are eating you out of existence!

Look at the Co-operatives! They are free of taxation. You are slaving for them!

Look at the Department Stores which are springing up like mushrooms all around you, and who double their profits from year to year. They will be your graves!

The result of all this is **cold socialisation.** – Marxism is guilty of pawning the German economy to international high finance. Therefore citizens, you belong to the ranks of those who make no pact with Marxism, but fight it wherever it is to be found.

German National Socialist Workers Party

offset the party's dismal showing in urban areas. In other words the NSDAP had found an unexpected reservoir of support in regions of small scale subsistence agriculture as well as in the market towns which depended upon rural industries and farming. With the recognition that the party would find little support from the working-class voter, the Nazi propaganda machine was overhauled and redirected towards the farming community and also towards 'the business man who is the most vigorous opponent of department stores and consumer co-operatives ... and the small shop-keeper who is already anti-Semitic' (Party correspondence; Dinklage to Stöhr, 14 December 1927). On 19 April Hitler officially 'clarified' the meaning of Article 17 of the Party Programme. Although this stated that here would be 'expropriation of land for communal purposes without compensation', Hitler explained that since the NSDAP accepted the principle of private property this clause referred merely to property illegally acquired or companies not run in accordance with the well-being of the community – that is, mainly Jewish speculative companies (*Völkische Beobachter*, 19 April 1928).

The re-alignment of party policy during 1928 brought new members into the party, although at first the increases were hardly spectacular. More important, a new leadership corps emerged, whose bureaucratic ability and absolute loyalty to Hitler meant that they were content with a managerial role within a rigid hierarchy and less prone to challenge the leadership over fundamental issues of party policy. Although few *Gauleiters* (regional leaders) as yet received a party salary, there was at least the promise of a seat in local or national parliaments, with all the privileges and status that this implied, and many were quick to seize the opportunity to enhance their own prestige by acquiring a party car (preferably a Mercedes) and any other perks which might be available.

The NSDAP was now a 'pyramid' organisation. At the summit all major political decisions were made by Hitler alone, although often in consultation with his advisors. Rudolf Hess was Hitler's indispensable right-hand man and personal secretary, whose administrative decisions were made 'in the name of the Führer'; while routine administration, in particular matters relating to finance, membership and propaganda, were dealt with by the Central Leadership (*Reichsleitung*) operating from Munich. Germany itself was divided into a number of *Gaus* (regions) each with a *Gauleiter* (region-leader) who was directly appointed by Hitler (the *Gauleiters* in turn attempted to bypass the Central Leadership by appealing directly to Hitler over any issue of conflict, and they squabbled like hens over the various crumbs of favour which fell from the Führer's table). Local branch leaders were appointed by the *Gauleiter*, and since the success of the *Gau* reflected upon the *Gauleiter*, he appointed local leaders most likely to further the fortunes of the party in a particular area, regardless of an individual's personal qualities, or lack of them. Finally the SA man, the common foot-slogger of the party, held up the base of the pyramid, risking life and limb for 'the Führer and Germany', but hoping in turn to hack his way up the hierarchy to a position of prestige and influence. And, just as Hitler's orders were passed down through the chain of command to the base, so information gathered locally on such issues as propaganda techniques, membership profiles, and intelligence reports on the activities of political opponents was relayed upwards to Munich, where it was processed and collated to inform future policy decisions.

During this period there was also an expansion of the NSDAP's horizontal structure: namely, those organisations which were designed to penetrate into rural areas and middle-class society. The National Socialist Students' League, the Hitler Youth, the National Socialist

Women's League and organisations such as the National Socialist Lawyers' Association, though superficially concerned with 'preservation of German values', were in fact specifically formed with the intention of undermining the confidence of the German *Mittelstand* in the institutions of Weimar democracy. Here indifference was translated into hostility, and hostility into forceful rejection of the entire 'system'. Thus in July 1928 Kurt Tempel lost his position as leader of the National Socialist Students' League and was replaced by Baldur von Schirach. Unlike Tempel, who had attempted to infuse egalitarian ideals into the League, von Schirach emphasised the traditional snob appeal of the Student Leagues, with their elitist pseudo-aristocratic duelling fraternities and beer-drinking clubs, and he purposefully stirred up ultra-nationalism and anti-Semitism inside the universities. The Hitler Youth, too, was reorganised. From being a recruiting ground for the Stormtroopers, it was made into a distinctive unit with all the military trappings and regalia of the armed forces, in which any 'nationalist-minded' father would be happy to enrol his young son.

Yet the 'problem' of the SA rumbled on. Although Hitler refrained from openly denouncing radical elements within the Stormtroops, he carefully distanced himself from their public attacks upon the 'reactionary *bourgeoisie*', and increasingly stressed the party's nationalism at the expense of socialism. Another tactic was to refuse speaking engagements in radical strongholds, so that much of the discussion and dispute over party policy was carried on in obscure party news-letters, not in the full glare of national publicity. Besides, Hitler was shrewd enough to realise that the Stormtroopers' idealism (even when it took politcally embarrassing forms) was an invaluable propaganda weapon in the hands of the party, which the other *bourgeois* parties could not match. And he well knew that sooner or later the National Socialists would have to confront the left-wing parties on their own ground if the NSDAP was ever to seize power in Germany. Such a final confrontation would require physical terror and mass intimidation – only his own SA men could be counted upon to perform such a task reliably.

Hitler Youth (and female admirer) in Meuselwitz.

A typical NSDAP 'public meeting', held in Glauchau, Saxony. Generally a fleet of lorries (loaned by a local businessman) would transport squads of SA men to the meeting place – normally the main square of the town or village. A party speaker would address the crowds, and afterwards there would be a procession led by the SA to the local war memorial to praise the dead of the First World War. Quite often a sympathetic pastor would lead a church service extolling the virtues of patriotism and sacrifice, and vilifying Marxist Social Democrats and 'Communism'. The purpose of such meetings was not so much to present policies to the electorate, as to present an image of strength, unity and respectability for the NSDAP.

The NSDAP combined the appeal of its essentially backward-looking ideology with a sharply scientific appreciation of the techniques of modern propaganda. In an era before the widespread use of the motion-picture for political purposes, and before radio could reach into every corner of the land, the NSDAP was beginning to perfect techniques of 'blanket propaganda'. Target areas were carefully selected by Himmler in Munich on the basis of very sophisticated analyses of graphs showing the relationships between population, membership growth, economic conditions and traditional patterns of political loyalty. A particular region would be selected, usually when an election was imminent, or a major NSDAP congress was about to be held, and the area was then blanketed with rallies and party meetings. Up to two hundred rallies might be held in the space of ten days and, in order to provide the necessary pool of public speakers, the party set up its own correspondence course to train members in the art of addressing meetings. Even sheets of set answers (approved by Hitler) were prepared in order to counter the inevitable uncomfortable questions about the real aims of National Socialism. Those who were drawn to the large rallies and then showed interest in the movement were invited to 'discussion evenings' in the village pub or local meeting hall, where they could meet local activists and be persuaded to join the party.

A new respectability

The 1929 National Socialist Party Congress took place in Nuremberg on the fifteenth anniversary of the outbreak of the First World War. At the Congress Hitler was particularly anxious to court the war-veterans' associations and the business community, and thereby maximise the political impact of the party among traditional right-wing voters. Once again discussion was kept to a minimum, and Hitler did not even bother to attend the various sessions concerned with debating the party's future course. The NSDAP leadership cadre now virtually mirrored the status divisions of German middle-class society, with educational qualifica-

tion increasing markedly in the upper echelons of the party. Among the Central Leadership Committee and the *Gauleiters* only three had what could be described as a working-class or 'poor' background, while nine were ex-white-collar staff, eight had been teachers, six senior civil servants and five officers in the Reichswehr. Moreover the party was at last in a position to expand its influence into urban areas – not into proletarian quarters but into the middle-class suburbs.

The fruits of the party's carefully cultivated image of respectability were apparent shortly after the 1929 Congress when Hitler unilaterally committed the NSDAP to cooperate with the German Nationalists (DNVP) and the *Stahlhelm* in a plebiscite against the Young Plan (an agreement to 'renegotiate' German reparation payments). Although many party functionaries were hostile to the idea of being associated with the party of Junker landlords and big business, they none the less accepted Hitler's decision. Equally there was no major internal party crisis when Hitler appeared on the same

Hitler receives the well-orchestrated adulation of the party at Nuremburg (left with bald head is Julius Streicher).

SOCIALISM?

That is the terrifying word that sends shivers down the back of every peaceful citizen.

Socialism, that means to him, **expropriation and equality**, **Jacobinery** and the **guillotine**.

Socialism, that means to him **Class-struggle**, because for 60 years the **Jew** has slyly put about this nonsense, both to the gullible worker and the ever-so-clever middle classes.

In reality **Socialism** means nothing other than **community: A people's community**.

Socialism can only originate from the principle of absolute justice: because without justice there is no community. But nothing is more unjust than equality, for man is in nature quite unequal. Man is not equal in fulfilling his duty, therefore he cannot be equal in his rights.

But he should not be valued according to his money, rather according to his accomplishments for the community. Whoever accomplishes the greatest service for his people, he shall be the first among us. But whoever thinks only of his money, he is a pariah and an outcast.

THE COMMON GOOD BEFORE INDIVIDUAL GREED
THAT IS SOCIALISM

Do you want to create a true and sound community within our German people, blooming with happiness and peace?

Then out with the swindle Marxism, and away with bourgeois selfishness!

Then join up with the party of the people's community.

German National Socialist Workers Party

An example of the NSDAP's new respectability – the pamphlet attempts to differentiate between 'Jewish socialism' and 'German socialism'.

public platform as Alfred Hugenberg – press lord, capitalist baron and the ultra-reactionary leader of the DNVP. And although the plebiscite campaign was politically inconsequential, it did much to reinforce the National Socialists' prestige among the *Mittelstand*, as well as swelling the party's coffers with contributions from business and commercial interests.

During the final days of the plebiscite campaign against the Young Plan an event occured which at the time provoked remarkably little comment in the National Socialist press, and whose long term

3.   The Rise of Fascism

Alfred Hugenberg. Managing director of Krupps Steel until 1917, Hugenberg controlled over 500 newspapers by the mid-1920s. In some provinces, such as Pomerania, only Hugenberg newspapers appeared. In 1926 he added Ufa (Universal Films) to his media empire, thereby extending his influence into the cinema. Hugenberg was appointed leader of the German Nationalist Party in October 1928.

Breakthrough!

The spectacular rise of Nazism after 1929 cannot simply be equated with the collapse of the German economy and the effects of mass unemployment. Certainly the Great Depression was an essential pre-condition for the rise of fascism in Germany, but it is necessary to examine *how* the NSDAP exploited political uncertainties and, particularly, middle-class fears in order to understand how Hitler seized power in 1933. After all, the rise of the German Communist Party during the recession was equally spectacular, and the Communists were by far the greatest beneficiaries of the discontent of the unemployed. It is even more noteworthy that Hitler was appointed Chancellor after the economic recession had peaked and after a national election in which the Nazis had actually lost two million votes.

During 1928 and 1929 the NSDAP scored a series of local and regional successes, but the party remained an essentially 'small-town phenomenon' unable to break out

Homeless and unemployed – a youth sleeps on the steps of a Berlin apartment block.

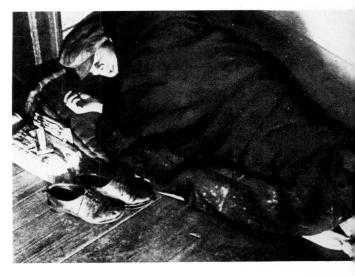

significance was at first missed by Hitler and the party leadership. At the end of October the New York Stock Market collapsed, wiping out billions of dollars worth of shares overnight, and sending financial shock waves around the world. In Germany unemployment, which dropped to a relative low-point of one and a quarter million in August 1929, reached three million by December and seemed set to reach four million by the end of 1930. On 31 October 1929 the first major German banking firm (the Beamtenbank) failed, and as huge queues of anxious savers formed outside the bank's closed doors, fears of another traumatic monetary crisis, similar to the hyper-inflation, began to grip the middle classes. The Great Depression had begun.

91

Homeless and unemployed – ex-steel workers pass the time in an inner-city hostel.

into the national scene. The first major test of the National Socalists' electoral strategy came in September 1930 when the German Chancellor Heinrich Brüning unexpectedly (and unnecessarily) called a general election. Brüning had been appointed Chancellor by President Hindenburg, in line with a section of the Weimar constitution which allowed the President to appoint a Chancellor, in the event of

---

The Great Depression

By 1932 German industrial production had fallen to just 59 per cent of its 1928 volume. Unemployment increased from 9.7 per cent in 1928 to 44.4 per cent in 1932.

	% of 'working population'		
	unemployed	short-time	full-time
1928	9.7	5.7	84.6
1930	22.7	13.8	63.5
1932	44.4	22.6	33.0

In 1930 alone, 40,000 small businesses collapsed. Unemployment benefits, originally paid for six months (after loss of employment), were cut to six weeks by June 1932. In 1932 over two million were forced to subsist on local authority welfare benefits which rarely covered even the cost of bread. The net weekly wage of industrial workers fell from approximately 42 RM per week in 1929 to 22 RM per week in 1932.
(*Sachwörterbuch der Geschichte Deutschlands*, Berlin 1969; D. Landes, *Der Entfesselte Prometheus,* Köln 1973).

A meeting of the Reichsbank on 15 November 1930 discusses the economic crisis.

PERSECUTION OF CHRISTIANS AND MURDER OF PRIESTS IN THE RUSSIAN PARADISE!

Up to 1928, 28 Bishops and 1200 priests murdered. Between 1928 and 1929 another 30 bishops and 1348 priests disappeared. Nothing more has been heard from them. Additionally thousands of other clergymen have died a martyr's death and thousands of nuns have been raped and murdered. At present 37,000 priests and over 8000 monks are languishing in the dungeons of the Tscheka or in the hell of Siberia. This report and a list of other repulsive atrocities, carried out by Bolshevik animals, was made public by the St. Elisabeth envoy in Nuremberg. The war is entirely directed against priests, nuns, the churches and schools. *Why this spiritual persecution*?

There are men who want to rule without God. Of them, Christ once said, 'The devil is their father. They are murderers from the outset. Hypocrites. Adders. These men are not like other men. In their secret texts they have set out how they will come to power, how they will come to rule the earth, how they will oppress the non-Jews. Their strategy is as follows:

The natural enemy of Israel is the christian church. Therefore it is necessary to destroy it. Its own divisions make the task easier. Support freethinking, doubt, disbelief and conflict. *Therefore constant war in the press against christian priests;* – promote suspicion, mock them. A major pillar of the church is the school. Gain influence over the christian upbringing of youth. *Split the churches from the schools.* Under the slogan of progress and equal treatment for all religions, change christian schools into confessionless (i.e. state) schools. Then Jewish teachers can work in all schools. Press for the abolition of all church and school property, its transfer to the state, therefore sooner or later into the hands of Israel.

BOLSHEVISM IS PERSECUTION OF CHRISTIANS BY THE JEWS!

Hundreds of thousands of examples could be given. So go to meetings of the National Socialists and hear the explanation. A leaflet is too small to set out all the various interconnections. Read anti-semitic newspapers and books, then check the facts by comparison with daily happenings! You can't change the Jew, any more than you can stop rust destroying iron. You can only keep it at bay. The Jew has to destroy. But you don't have to put up with his destruction.

First the monarchy must be abolished, then the military. After that the spiritual leaders and intelligentsia. Then the Jew is master and we the slaves – circus animals, beasts of burden for the Jews.

If you want that to happen, then stay with the present-day parties, who don't want to suppress this Jewish mania; then carry on reading those newspapers which remain silent about all this. If you want things to change though, then fight with our leaders for a Germany under German leadership, join the

NATIONAL SOCIALIST GERMAN WORKERS PARTY – Vote for List 9.

Reichstag Election
14.9.1930

political stalemate in the Reichstag. In effect, Brüning (a member of the Catholic Centre Party) was able to rule by Presidential decree and had no immediate need of a parliamentary majority to carry through his programme. Nevertheless his massively deflationary policies, which included the lowering of the already meagre levels of unemployment benefit, cuts in public services and reductions in civil servants' pay were highly unpopular, and brought about a politicisation of all segments of society in an attempt to defend living standards.

The election results brought startling confirmation of the growing popularity of the National Socialists among the German middle classes. The NSDAP secured 107 seats in the Reichstag, obtained 6.4 million votes, and increased its share of the poll from 3.6 per cent (May 1928) to 18.3 per cent. Not unexpectedly the Nazis obtained their best results in the countryside and from lower-middle-class voters in the north. But most significantly the party for the first time managed to penetrate into large urban areas, and even gained some limited support in working-class districts. In Berlin, for example, the NSDAP polled 9 per cent in the radical proletarian quarter of Wedding, 26 per cent in middle-class Steglitz and nearly 18 per cent in affluent Zehlendorf. The results demonstrated conclusively that avowedly 'apolitical' middle-class Germans would cling desperately to their social and economic privileges at a time of falling living standards, and respond fanatically to a programme which promised both the annihilation of political opponents and the appointment of a dictator to guarantee middle-class interests.

The immediate task for the party leadership, in the wake of the 14 September election results which lifted the party from relative insignificance to become the second largest party in the Reichstag, was to convert electoral approval into a passionate identification with the cult of Adolf Hitler and Nazism. Sympathisers needed to be integrated into the party structure and thoroughly indoctrinated in the values of National Socialism. A far less desirable by-product of success, however, was the sudden exposure of the NSDAP's political programme to wide-spread scrutiny and analysis. The frequently contradictory nature of the party's policies often became uncomfortably apparent, while the sudden expectation of power made it even more difficult to suppress internal conflicts by appealing to the myth of the Führer's infallibility. Thus when party officials in Saxony went on record to express the NSDAP's 'absolute opposition to any form of industrial sabotage' (i.e. strikes), National Socialists in Berlin were expressing their 'unconditional solidarity with the workers' by vigorously supporting a metal workers' strike for higher wages. Indeed the election breakthrough left the party in real danger of disintegrating into a series of feuding empires, each jealously ruled by a bureaucratic war-lord whose retinue of soldiers and camp-followers sought to ingratiate themselves into the movement for future financial rewards.

Rebellion in the SA

Immediately after the September elections the smouldering discontent within the ranks of the SA burst into open conflict when the Berlin Stormtroopers went on strike and refused to protect party meetings. Although superficially the crisis was provoked by a disagreement over finance between Goebbels and Walter Stennes (the SA leader of Berlin and Eastern Germany), in fact the conflict concerned much more fundamental issues: namely, the debate over the NSDAP's now openly reactionary tendencies and the role of the Stormtroopers within the party. Otto Strasser (the brother of the high-ranking party leader Gregor Strasser) had already quarrelled publicly with Hitler over the NSDAP's links with big business and its courting of the aristocracy. And although Otto did not have the status of his brother

Walter Stennes (in white coat) shortly before his dismissal from the SA.

Gregor within the National Socialist movement, his open clash had the effect of fanning the discontent of the lowly party foot-soldiers with their high-living generals.

In response to the open rebellion, Hitler rushed to Berlin and confronted the rebels. He calmed the mutiny by appointing himself leader of the SA (the previous head of the SA, Franz von Pfeffer, had 'resigned' in August) and promised to look into complaints about the party's administration personally. During the final part of 1930 the uneasy truce held, and Hitler attempted to consolidate the peace by appointing Ernst Röhm as SA Chief of Staff in the New Year (Röhm had played a leading role in the abortive Munich putsch of 1923, after which he spent some time in Bolivia on behalf of the German army). It was hoped that Röhm's close contacts with the Reichswehr would reassure the Conservative establishment, while his military background and radical tendencies would reassure the SA that they would not be overlooked when the time came to share out the spoils of power.

Despite Röhm's attempts to curb the independence of SA units, substantial grievances remained, particularly as the political unreliability of the Stormtroopers persuaded Hitler to place greater emphasis upon the rival SS organisation, which had remained steadfastly loyal during the Berlin crisis. The SS was therefore expanded at the expense of the SA and its image as a praetorian guard carefully embellished – an image that contrasted strongly with the dangerously radical, anti-bourgeois ethos of many SA units. But when, on 20 February 1931, Hitler issued an order forbidding the SA to engage in street-fighting as proof of his party's policy of 'legality', it proved to be the last straw. To the rank and file Stormtroopers, many of whom were unemployed and penniless, this was the final compromise with the hated 'system'. In Berlin there were instances of wholesale defection to the Communists and when, at the end of March Walter Stennes was suspended for failing to co-operate with the authorities, a second and more serious rebellion occured.

This time Hitler's response was brutal. Convincing himself that Stennes could only be a police spy, he dismissed him from the party and temporarily dissolved the entire SA while Göring conducted a thorough purge. There were cuts in the SA's budget and for a time no new applications for membership of the SA were accepted. (The SS was in the meantime expanded.) Finally, all appointments to the SA's staff were put under the control of a party functionary and a Reich's Leader-

Berlin 8 April 1931
Collapse!

Betrayal by the party clique ... How often have we denounced the betrayal of National Socialism by our 'bosses', in the desperate hope of being able to turn around the rudder of our freedom movement ...?

... Hitler and his circle have made the party a cesspool of dried-up bourgeois bankrupts. While we, the committed party activists, must hold the reins for the ambitious betrayers who still devote themselves completely to capitalism, so that they can fulfill their long cherished dream of becoming cabinet ministers at the age of forty.

So we can starve? Like Hell!

... Do you remember how Hitler commended the Ulmer officers, Scheringer, Wendt and Ludin, saying that they were upright German men? Well Scheringer's resignation hit the party like a bomb, while in the meantime Wendt had also left the party and was standing openly against Hitler. Hitler paled and almost collapsed when Scheringer threw the 'irrevocable' party programme in his face with the words, "You have obviously given up socialism within the last few months. You have spoken reverently of capitalism. In domestic politics and economic discussions you have looked after the interests of big capital as opposed to the interests of the middle classes, the small farmers and the deep suffering working class. You have voted against the removal of the Young Plan. You have nurtured inside the party a Byzantine ethic which stinks!"

What a miserable attempt to refute this proven betrayal of the National Socialist idea, when the Völkischer Beobachter wrote in Number 83 on March 24th 1931, that "abolition of the capitalist system has for centuries been nothing more than a catchphrase."

Can there be a more grotesque betrayal of socialism?

The blush of shame must surely come to the faces of Hitler and his bosses. With this betrayal Hitler has declared himself conclusively for the programme of the bourgeois parties who are already disintegrating, and has created an abysmal chasm between the party and the millions of farmers and trades people and workers ...

Party Comrades! SA Comrades! National Socialists! It is not just a question of Röhm, Goebbels or even Hitler!

It is a question of the goal of our movement! Protect our old ideals!

Do not stand for the betrayal of socialism by selfish politicians, for whom the party is an end in itself!

The common good comes before self-interest!

It is a question of the freedom of our people. Not of treacherous bosses!

Several National Socialist and SA comrades

ship School was established in a thinly disguised attempt to indoctrinate SA leaders and weed out potential 'trouble-makers'.

The Berlin mutiny clearly demonstrated the danger that the scramble for power would unmask the true face of Nazism, and in order to counter this danger Hitler appointed Goebbels as overlord of the Reich's Propaganda Leadership early in 1931. Under Goebbels' leadership propaganda activities were controlled and centralised to an extent never before conceived. Local areas were forbidden to undertake independent campaigns, while political propaganda was transmitted in a pre-determined and pre-packaged form throughout Germany in line with Goebbels' analysis of the national situation. Even campaigns aimed at vilifying political opponents were orchestrated from Berlin to the extent of specifying the size and colour of propaganda posters and leaflets. Any departures from Goebbels' directives were considered grave breaches of party discipline, and those responsible faced expulsion.

The worm in the bud: Nazi 'co-ordination' of political institutions

The Nazis' attack upon the Weimar political system was not confined to the attempt to gain power through the ballot box. Certainly electoral popularity was an important yardstick with which to measure National Socialism's success in destabilising parliamentary democracy, for Hitler boasted that a vote for his party was a vote against 'government by sheep' and in favour of a strong authoritarian state. But equally important in preparing the way for

Two examples of Nazi propaganda directed towards the commercial middle classes. The turnover of small shops (*Einzelhandel*) fell from 36.3 billion RM in 1928 to 33.1 billion RM in 1930 and to just 23.1 billion RM in 1932. *Above* The 'Jewish Department Store Octopus' eats up small German traders. *Below* 'Christmas is a christian festival'. The leaflet implores its readers to buy at German shops, and not to shop at Christmas in Jewish department stores.

a seizure of power *after* a constitutional hand-over of government to the NSDAP, was the tactic of undermining the very foundations of a pluralist society by 'co-ordination' of important political institutions (the German word *Gleichschaltung* is difficult to translate into English, but is usually termed 'co-ordination'). The NSDAP therefore set out to infiltrate any group which could influence political decision-making, especially those groups which represented middle-class interests, by flooding the membership with party members and replacing independent spokesmen with dedicated Nazis.

The most successful campaign of co-ordination was masterminded by Walter Darré and his so-called Agricultural Office, which within a matter of months after its establishment had totally crippled the independence of the farmers' pressure group, the *Landbund*, and made it into a sounding board for Nazi doctrine. Among the urban middle classes, particularly those whose trade was severely affected by the Great Depression, the NSDAP established the Militant Association of Retailers. The Association agitated against large department stores and consumer co-operatives, accusing them of being 'agents of Jewish Stock Exchange capitalism' who were responsible for the demise of small traders and shopkeepers. Furthermore, the Association promised that under the Third Reich there would be a return to a form of medieval guild-economy in which competition would be controlled by corporate bodies, in place of an economic system determined by free market forces. Yet here again the blatantly opportunistic nature of the NSDAP's politics was often exposed by its very success. Thus when Wilhelm Kube demanded in the Prussian parliament that the SPD should distribute free firewood to the poor, Walter Darré was elsewhere demanding that wood prices should be increased to give foresters a better wage! Despite such embarrassments, however, the internal disintegration of Weimar democracy was well advanced by the second

half of 1931, with parasitic Nazi cells multiplying in almost every organ of the state, including the civil service, the teaching profession and the armed forces. Even more sinister was Himmler's success in placing high-ranking Nazis in the police forces of Berlin and Bavaria.

The Harzburg front

On 11 October 1931 Hitler appeared together with leaders of the German Nationalists, right-wing veterans' associations and the leading figures of German heavy industry and agriculture in Harzburg, for what was supposed to be a joint right-wing protest against the Brüning government. The day before Hitler had met President Hindenburg for the first time, confidently believing that he could persuade the ageing president to appoint him Chancellor of a right-wing coalition government. Sadly for Hitler, the old field-marshal was singularly unimpressed by the *petit bourgeois* mannerisms of the 'bohemian corporal', remarking that Hitler might be suitable as the Minister of Posts, but was not fitted to be Chancellor of Greater Germany. And in Harzburg the presence of so many decorous and distinguished members of the aristocracy clearly unnerved Hitler. Affronted by the patronising behaviour of his allies, he publicly snubbed his partners by leaving the reviewing stand after the march-past of his own SA and before the parade of the other formations.

A week later the NSDAP staged its own massive propaganda rally with 100,000 SA men in the state capital of Brunswick, as if to underline the suggestion that the National Socialist movement alone was strong enough to topple the Weimar state. Fortified by further election victories and continuing spectacular increases in party membership, Hitler told the SA and the SS in December: 'The movement is approaching the last hour of the march.' 1932, he confidently predicted, would be 'the first year of the Third Reich'.

The Harzburg Front was a coalition of the NSDAP, the DNVP and the right-wing paramilitary organisation, the *Stahlhelm*. Also included were representatives of heavy industry including Thyssen and Vögler, the *Junker Reichslandbund* under Graf Kalckreuth, the All German League, the League of the Fatherland under General van der Goltz, the (Hohenzollern) Prince Frederick of Prussia and army generals von Seeckt and Lüttwitz. *Above* The *Stahlhelm* gather in Munich for a massive demonstration. *Below* Hugenberg and other dignitaries watch the parade of the SA at Harzburg. Shortly afterwards Hitler left the scene.

The last hour of the march

As it turned out, 1932 was not the first year of the Third Reich, but rather twelve months of expectancy, frustration and anguish for Hitler and the National Socialist movement. It was marked by the desperate campaign for the Presidency in March and April; the high point of the 31 July election victory in which the NSDAP polled 13.7 million votes; and the formidable set-back of the November elections which plunged many National Socialist leaders, including Goebbels, into despair. And yet on 30 January 1933 President Hindenburg appointed Hitler Chancellor despite the consistent doubts and misgivings he had voiced throughout 1932. How could this happen?

Hitler achieved power by reason of a complex series of backroom intrigues and conspiracies. The millions of votes and the tens of thousands of Stormtroops which he commanded could, of themselves, never have propelled him to power, for the NSDAP had no prospects of gaining an absolute majority in the German Reichstag (in free and fair elections), nor was Hitler willing to risk a second confrontation with the army by attempting an armed putsch. Instead, the 'forces' which Hitler commanded were used as the bishops and knights in a deadly game of political chess – a game which demanded the greatest reserves of nerve and tenacity, but in which Hitler's genius as a master tactician proved crucial. Indeed, although the Nazi seizure of power in 1933 displayed all the hallmarks of a *coup d'état*, it was a 'constitutional' *coup d'état* in which naked terror was masked by the appearance of legality. Hitler had taken to heart the lesson of November 1923.

By 1930 the presidential palace was the real centre of political power in Germany. The effective stalemate of the parties in the Reichstag allowed the President to use his exceptional powers under Article 48 of the constitution to appoint chancellors, and he enabled them to carry out their programmes through presidential decree. Naturally those close to the eighty-four-year-old President were in a position decisively to influence the course of German politics, and the retinue round Hindenburg was akin to a medieval court, with the many factions intriguing and conspiring to further their particular interests. In a politically astute move, a group of wealthy industrialists and landowners made a gift of the large estate of Neudeck to Hindenburg on his eightieth birthday. Therefore, in line with his military background and his newly acquired aristocratic airs, Hindenburg surrounded himself with army officers, Junker landowners and industrialists. Among these, two individuals in particular stood out. One was the President's son, Oskar von Hindenburg, to whose advice the old man usually yielded in a time of crisis or uncertainty. The other was the scheming commander of the armed forces, General Schleicher, who in turn exercised considerable influence upon Oskar.

It was Schleicher who had been primarily responsible for Brüning's appointment to the Chancellorship in March 1930 after the collapse of the Great Coalition led by Hermann Müller of the SPD. And despite the electoral verdict upon Brüning's government in September 1930, Brüning was able to survive with Hindenburg's support (and the 'toleration' of the SPD) until 1932. Brüning himself, although an aloof and inept politician, had qualities which commended him to the President. He was an honest and capable administrator in the traditional bureaucratic mould of the German civil servant. He was *not* a member of the Social Democratic Party. And he represented and cherished the same archaic conservative values of 'old Germany' as the ancient field marshal himself. Lastly, precisely because of his background, Brüning was hostile to the *petit bourgeois* radicalism and demagogy of Hitler and the

NSDAP, which he saw as a threat to the power of the established army and a potential obstacle to the stabilisation of a right-wing presidential dictatorship. By the same measure, however, Brüning was ill-equipped to survive the intrigues of the presidential court, and he was certainly no match for Schleicher's particular brand of double-dealing.

Whatever his failings as a politician, Brüning recognised the threat that the Nazis posed, and he put into operation a number of repressive measures to combat them. But, unknown to Brüning, Schleicher was simultaneously cautioning the President and the Minister of Defence (General Groener) against suppressing a populist right-wing movement which was a fanatical opponent of Marxism, and which might provide the army with a valuable reserve militia. Thus Schleicher began his campaign to 'integrate' the National Socialist movement into the structure of traditional right-wing politics. His aim was to harness the NSDAP's energy and popularity in such a way as to neutralise Hitler's totalitarian ambitions.

The game of cat-and-mouse between Schleicher and Hitler – in which Schleicher played mouse in the sad delusion that he was the cat – began in January 1932. Hitler was suddenly summoned to Berlin to conduct talks with Brüning and Schleicher over the possibility of extending Hindenburg's seven-year term without the necessity of a dangerously divisive presidential election. (On receiving the invitation in Munich to enter negotiations, Hitler is reported to have screamed with satisfaction. Then, having peered into the faces of his assembled entourage, he banged the telegram on the table and shouted, 'Now I have them in my pocket. They have recognised me as a partner in their negotiations.') In return for Hitler's support for such a proposal (allowable if two thirds of the Reichstag agreed), Brüning offered to resign once new reparation negotiations had been settled and hinted that he would urge Hindenburg to appoint Hitler as his replacement. Gregor Strasser urged Hitler to go along with the proposal, predicting that Hindenburg could not be beaten in an election contest. But Röhm and Goebbels disagreed, arguing that the NSDAP should not tie its hands in such a manner, and urging Hitler to stand for the presidency himself. Hitler in fact rejected Brüning's proposal, but the decision to announce himself as a presidential candidate cost him a month of anguish, for he feared that defeat would rupture his followers' belief in the invincibility of the NSDAP and their Führer.

In the middle of this month of indecision Hitler spoke at a meeting in Düsseldorf, the centre of the German steel industry. He had been invited to address an audience of important business leaders and industrial magnates whose enthusiasm for National Socialism had decidedly cooled on account of the numerous radical and 'socialist' pronouncements being made by SA units in the large cities. In a two-and-a-half hour monologue Hitler ranged across the whole spectrum of his views, although he was careful to concentrate upon the doctrine of the 'survival of the fittest'. That meant, he stated, 'the recognition of unequal achievement in both the political and economic spheres'. Democracy and communism were false values which must be destroyed and replaced with a belief in the 'inner value' of Germany and the 'sanctity' of private property. 'Today we are at a turning point,' he told his audience. 'Either we shall succeed ... or Germany will fall in final ruin.' (M. Domarus, *Hitler. Reden und Proklamationen, 1932-1945*, Bd. 1. Würzburg 1962). As he sat down, the audience rose to their feet to applaud. Much more important, however, they agreed to provide the finance that the NSDAP desperately needed to pay for its minutely planned and expensively staged presidential campaign.

Despite the technical brilliance of the NSDAP's presidential campaign, Hindenburg achieved a comfortable victory in the run-off on 10 April. Three days later

Brüning was able to extend the temporary ban on the SS and SA announced in March by imposing a formal dissolution on the grounds that the Stormtroops had planned to launch a *coup d'état* in the event of a Hitler victory. Certainly Röhm was tempted, for the SA's four hundred thousand men outnumbered the regular army by four to one. Hitler, however, refused to be provoked, and in disgust Röhm began his own secret negotiations with General Schleicher with the aim of creating an SA-dominated state militia. Röhm's apparent readiness to compromise persuaded Schleicher that it might be possible to split the 'reasonable' wing of the NSDAP from its political leadership – the unyielding triumvirate of Hitler, Goebbels and Göring. And as a first step in this policy, he needed to have the ban on the SA and the SS lifted.

Schleicher first of all used his influence with the President to put pressure on General Groener, who had signed the order to ban the NSDAP para-military organisations, to ban the republican *Reichsbanner* as well. Then, after leaking an internal document from Groener's own Ministry of Defence implying that Groener favoured the republican side at the expense of the Nazis, Schleicher so discredited Groener that he was able to force his resignation. The loss of Groener left Brüning seriously exposed, and with Hindenburg's position as President now secure, Schleicher and his associates moved in for the kill. One of the Brüning cabinet's suggestions had been to settle landless labourers on some of the huge insolvent aristocratic estates in eastern Prussia. At Schleicher's instigation a group of Junker landlords went to visit Hindenburg at his Neudeck estate, and demanded Brüning's dismissal for advocating 'agrarian bolshevism'. Immediately afterwards Schleicher announced that Brüning no longer had the support of the army in his policy of suppressing the SA, and on 20 May Hindenburg announced Brüning's dismissal.

Schleicher's choice for the now vacant post of Chancellor was Franz von Papen – a smooth, distinguished and ambitious aristocrat with family connections to both French and German big business, who commended himself to the President on account of his reactionary political views and his flattery. But von Papen's appointment was not mere chance. On the day of Brüning's dismissal Hitler was summoned to a second meeting with the President where he was asked if he would support von Papen in the event of Brüning's departure. Hitler tersely confirmed the bargain that he had struck with Schleicher; namely that he would 'tolerate' von Papen in return for a lifting of the ban on the SA and the SS and the dissolution of the Reichstag.

In the event von Papen had great difficulty in forming a cabinet which included any notable political figures. Eventually the 'cabinet of barons', as it became known, included seven aristocrats of established right-wing views, a minister of economics borrowed from the chemical conglomerate IG Farben, a minister of labour who was the director of Krupps, and a minister of justice from Bavaria whose only previous action of note had been to protect Hitler from prosecution during his early political career. The British ambassador wrote to London on 14 April: 'The present cabinet is a cabinet of mutual deception.'

At the end of June the ban on the SA was finally lifted by von Papen. During the next month a wave of political violence claimed the lives of eighty-six persons. The fiercest battles were between Communists and Nazis, as each side responded to provocations and demonstrations by their political opponents. Yet despite the level of street violence, the greatest blow to the already shaky legal foundations of the state was struck by von Papen himself, when on 20 July, just ten days before the Reichstag elections, he used emergency powers to depose the Prussian government. Prussia was the last stronghold of the Social Democracy, and thus the bastion of

Political violence was endemic throughout the period of the Weimar Republic, but during the final months of 1932 violent confrontation between political opponents claimed hundreds of lives – not only in brutal street battles but in the cold-blooded murder of political opponents. *Above* Brüning's first measure to counteract political violence on 8 December 1930 was to ban the wearing of political uniforms. The SA responded by marching in shirts and ties. The banner reads: 'The sheep bleats. The cow laughs. Because shirts are dangerous to the state.' *Below* Police clear the streets during Reichstag elections in Berlin.

Above The aftermath of an SA attack on a
Communist meeting in the working-class district of
Wedding, Berlin. *Below* Poisonous political
propaganda created an atmosphere of terror and
hatred. A Nazi propaganda leaflet attacks the KPD:
'Fight with us against the Bolshevik blood-terror'.
The illustrations show the Communists burning
farms, sabotaging the railways, storing arms and
murdering opponents.

Freiwillige Arbeitsdienſtpflicht der K. P. D.

In uneigennütziger Weiſe iſt man den Bauern
beim Trocknen der Ernte behilflich —

Dem Verkehrsweſen und einer raſcheren Beförderung
von Reiſenden dienen beſondere Ausſchüſſe —

Keine Nachtſchicht und keine Überſtunde werden
geſcheut, um nützliche Gegenſtände unter Dach und
Fach zu bringen —

Im übrigen wird die vaterländiſche Ertüchtigung
durch fleißiges Scheibenſchießen gefördert.

Kämpft mit uns gegen
bolſchewiſtiſchen Blutterror! **Wählt Liſte 13**
Nationalſozialiſtiſche Deutſche Arbeiterpartei (Hitlerbewegung)

organised working-class opposition to the
far-right. While the workers mobilised for
the political strike which must inevitably
follow such a blatantly unconstitutional
act, the SPD leadership equivocated,
fearing to unleash what might become a
civil war. In the end they failed to act, and
yielded to what they saw as 'force majeur'.
It was effectively the last chance to rally
the working class to the defence of democracy and the republic.

The July election results brought the
NSDAP and its followers to a fever pitch of
expectancy and euphoria. Yet once again
the NSDAP could not gain an absolute
majority although it had more than
doubled its support in comparison with the
elections of September 1930. None the less,
as leader of the largest party in the
Reichstag, Hitler put a series of uncom-
promising proposals to Schleicher and
Hindenburg. He demanded the post of
Chancellor for himself and leading cabinet
positions for National Socialists, although
he would accept Schleicher as minister of
defence. The Führer retired to the
mountain air of Berchtesgaden and
awaited the summons to the presidential
palace. When the invitation finally arrived,
however, he found himself confronted by
an equally unyielding Hindenburg, who
offered him the vice-chancellorship but
refused to dismiss von Papen. Hitler,
barely able to conceal his anger and
disappointment, tartly turned the offer
down.

During August there were discussions
between the NSDAP and the Centre Party
over the possibility of forming a coalition
government which could command
majority support in the Reichstag. Though
the negotiations did not succeed, an
informal alliance was struck which led to
Göring's election as President of the
Reichstag. Shortly afterwards there
followed a farcical attempt to oust von
Papen from the Chancellorship. A motion
of no-confidence in von Papen's cabinet
was tabled which was passed as von Papen

Above A motorised column of Nationalists in para-military uniform threatens a marching column of *Reichsbanner* (SPD) members.

Below NSDAP branch at Atzendorf, near Magdeburg, in 1932. Those present are typically small farmers and members of the *Mittelstand*.

GERMAN FARMER
YOU BELONG TO HITLER!
WHY?

The German farmer stands in between two great dangers today:

The one danger is the American economic system — Big capitalism!

it means 'world economic crisis'
it means 'eternal interest slavery' ...
it means that the world is nothing more than a bag of booty for Jewish finance in Wall Street,
    New York and Paris
it enslaves man under the slogans of progress, technology, rationalisation, standardisation,
    etc.
it knows only profit and dividends
it wants to make the world into a giant trust
it puts the machine over man
it annihilates the independent earth-rooted farmer, and its final aim is the world dictatorship
    of Jewry ...

it achieves this in the political sphere, through parliament and the swindle of democracy. In
    the economic sphere, through the control of credit, the mortgaging of land, the Stock
    Exchange and the Market principle ...
The Farmer's Leagues, the Landvolk and the Bavarian Farmers' League all pay homage
    to this system.

The other danger is the Marxist economic system of BOLSHEVISM:

it knows only the State economy
it knows only one class, the proletariat
it brings in the controlled economy
it doesn't just annihilate the self-sufficient farmer economically — it roots him out ...
it brings the rule of the tractor
it nationalises the land and creates mammoth factory-farms
it uproots and destroys man's soul, making him the powerless tool of the communist idea —
    or kills him
it destroys the family, belief and customs ...
it is anti-Christ, it desecrates the churches ...

its final aim is the world-dictatorship of the proletariat, that means ultimately the world
    dictatorship of Jewry, for the Jew controls this powerless proletariat and uses it for his
    dark plans

Big Capitalism and Bolshevism work hand in hand; they are born of Jewish thought and
    serve the master plan of world Jewry.

Who alone can rescue the farmer from these dangers?

NATIONAL SOCIALISM!

A leaflet appealing to farmers, produced for the first round of the Presidential election in 1932.

himself presented a presidential decree dissolving the Reichstag. Whatever the intentions of the Nazi leadership, the effect was to plunge the NSDAP into its fifth major election campaign of the year. This time, though, as von Papen had gambled, the Nazis suffered a severe setback, with their total percentage of the vote dropping from 37.3 to 33.1. It seemed as if the Nazi tide had reached its high-point in July, and was now receding. And yet the peaking of the Nazi vote was, ironically, the event which check-mated the attempts of the conservative establishment to neutralise Hitler, for just as the NSDAP lost two million votes, the Communists had increased their share to nearly six million. Schleicher's policy of bringing Hitler's brown-shirted battalions into a right-wing nationalist coalition was no longer a political 'option' for the conservative establishment – it was an immediate and pressing necessity.

In late November, two weeks after the Reichstag elections, a group of prominent industrialists, including Thyssen, Krupp, Siemens, Bosch and Schacht, put pressure on Hindenburg to create some form of authoritarian nationalist regime with mass support. Such a regime, they argued, would be a counter-weight to the threat posed by the KPD and was necessary to ensure Germany's 'economic survival'. In effect it was a plea to Hindenburg to trust Hitler, for the industrialists wrote: 'We recognise in the national movement which has penetrated our people the beginning of an era, which through the overcoming of class contrasts, creates the essential basis for a rebirth of the German economy.' (Document PS 3901, Nuremberg Trials).

Schleicher, however, had no intention of deserting the political arena. Nor indeed had von Papen, who on 1 December urged Hindenburg to reappoint him Chancellor with powers to rule under a state of emer-gency. At first Hindenburg showed willing to reappoint von Papen, but Schleicher intervened to warn the President that such a course would provoke a civil war which the army would be powerless to control. Instead Schleicher offered to form his own cabinet with substantial Nazi backing (which could gain a Reichstag majority) by splitting the NSDAP and taking the 'moderate' wing under Gregor Strasser into the government. The next day Schleicher was himself appointed Chancellor.

In effect Schleicher had finally been flushed out into the open and forced to gamble on the chance that Strasser would be able to prise away a substantial section of the NSDAP from Hitler's leadership. Certainly spirits among the rank and file and within the lower echelons of the Nazi party were low. Interminable election campaigns and the exhortation to repeated sacrifices in the name of the Führer did not seem to be bringing tangible rewards. But Schleicher did not understand that the very foundations of the party had been painstakingly constructed by Hitler precisely to withstand such a period of strain, and that Strasser had neither the organisational basis nor the charismatic qualities to exploit this discontent. When Strasser found himself unable to convince his colleagues that some form of compromise with the system was essential, he simply caved in, and far from attempting to lead a rebellion against Hitler's leadership, he resigned from the party and fled Berlin for Italy.

Yet Schleicher still blindly believed that he could create a cabinet of 'national consensus' by promising to create work and claiming to represent 'neither socialism nor capitalism'. He therefore made an opening to the left by reviving the plan to settle 800,000 acres of the eastern estates, and sought to make some sort of deal with the trade unions on wages and job creation. Then, in a final fatal move, he threatened to make public a secret Reichstag report on the *Osthilfe* scandal, which would show how corrupt Junkers had milked tax

GERMAN WOMEN! GERMAN MOTHERS!
GERMAN WOMEN! GERMAN MOTHERS!

Our Young people Defiled:

Dr. Zacharias, Dresden, reports as follows:

The present Prussian Welfare Minister Hirtsiefer has confirmed after questions were asked, that in a German Grammar School for Girls 63% of the girls had experienced sexual intercourse and 47% had some form of sexual disease ...

The number of sexual offences and cases of incest pile up in the most gruesome manner! Since January 1st 1932, 92 convictions against sex offenders have been reported, of which 12 cases were incest, 5 of sexual murder, 40 offences against children and 35 were offences against adults.

This is a result of the many years during which our people, and in particular our youth, have been exposed to a flood of muck and filth, in word and print, in the theatre and in the cinema. These are the results of the systematic Marxist destruction of the family. And all this despite the fact that we have a chancellor of the 'Christian Centre Party', and despite the fact of a Hindenberg, who as President watches over the constitution, which according to Article 122 is supposed to protect our youth against spiritual, bodily and moral harm.

Is there no possibility of salvation? Must our people, our youth, sink without hope of rescue into the muck and filth? No!!! The National Socialists must win the election so that they can put a halt to this Marxist handiwork, so that once again women are honoured and valued, and so that the cinema and the theatre contributes to the inner rebuilding of the nation.

German women and mothers. Do you want your honour to sink still further?

Do you want your daughters to be playthings and the objects of sexual lust?

IF NOT then vote for a National Socialist Majority on JULY 31st.

Then vote for

LIST TWO
HITLER-MOVEMENT   NAT. SOCIAL GERMAN
WORKERS PARTY

Leaflet produced for the Reichstag elections, 31 July 1932.

allowances and subsidies from the state and spirited the money into their private coffers. (Hindenburg was also implicated in this scandal, and fear of exposure largely accounts for his 'about-turn' in appointing Hitler Chancellor at the end of January). Right-wing support for Schleicher evaporated almost overnight.

On 4 January 1933 Hitler and von Papen met in secret at the house of the banker Kurt von Schroeder, together with the industrialists who had signed the letter to Hindenburg pressing for Hitler to be taken into the government. Although the various participants have since given conflicting and contradictory accounts of what was agreed, there can be little doubt that this meeting paved the way for Hitler's accession to the Chancellorship of a great nationalist coalition. Certainly at the end of the meeting the NSDAP's chronic financial debts were mysteriously paid off, and Goebbels recorded in his diary on the 5th: 'The present government knows that this is the end for them.' Naturally the partners were still at the bargaining stage, and with this in mind the Nazis threw every ounce of their strength and prestige into local elections in the tiny constituency of Lippe on 15 January. The

'success' that the NSDAP scored (at the expense of the traditional right-wing parties) revived the impetus of the NSDAP's forward march, and put further pressure on the conservatives to reach a rapid agreement with Hitler.

Schleicher made his last vain bid to hold on to power at the end of January by appealing to Hindenburg to dissolve the Reichstag and rule by presidential decree. In effect this would have meant a military dictatorship based upon the bayonets of the Reichswehr. But Hindenburg was not yet so senile as not to recognise that Schleicher was contradicting the advice he had given on 2 December. If, as he had then argued, the army could not guarantee order in the event of civil war, how could Schleicher press for a military dictatorship when the political situation had, if anything, become more critical? Schleicher had no answer, and within a few days he too had fallen victim to behind the scenes conspiracies – this time between von Papen and Hitler.

Finally on Monday, 30 January, after a

Under police protection Nazi Stormtroopers parade outside the headquarters of the KPD (Karl Liebknecht House) on 22 January 1933.

sleepless night and a last-minute display of calculated brinkmanship, Hitler received the summons to meet the President in his office. When he emerged, it was as Chancellor of Germany in a right-wing nationalist cabinet in which the NSDAP, on the face of it, seemed sparsely represented. Many of the members of the von Papen and Schleicher cabinets remained in their posts. Von Papen himself was Vice-chancellor and also Minister President of Prussia; Hugenberg held the position of Minister of Economics and Agriculture; while the leader of the Stahlhelm, Franz Seldte, was appointed Minister of Labour. In many respects it was the old cabinet of barons with a populist image, and these same barons confidently predicted that they had at last succeeded in taming the wild man of German politics and made him a prisoner of *their* system. What they failed to understand was that *their* system was in a state of chronic inner decay, and Hitler's appointment to the Chancellorship was a hammer-blow to the structure which caused its final collapse.

4

The Last Act

Those who forget the past
Will be condemned
To relive it in the future.
(Santayana)

In the November 1932 elections the combined vote of the Social Democratic and Communist parties numbered 13,228,000 compared to a total of 14,696,000 recorded for the Nazis and the German Nationalists. In numerical terms, then, the proletarian parties were almost as strong as their political opponents on the far right. And, given the level of working-class political organisation, particularly in the trade union movement, the left should have been capable of defending itself against any sustained assault by the far right. Yet less than twelve months after the November 1932 elections – elections which apparently dealt a severe blow to the Nazis – the political, economic and cultural organisations created by three generations of German workers lay in ruins, while the entire leadership cadre of the SPD and the KPD, together with the cream of the German intelligentsia, languished in the barbed-wire compounds of concentration camps, or had been driven into exile.

'Social fascism'

Not long after the failure of the German Communist uprising of 1923, Joseph Stalin wrote that fascism and social democracy were 'twins', in that both placed themselves at the disposal of the *bourgeoisie* in the political struggle to crush the revolutionary working class. At the Fourth World

Congress of the Communist International (Comintern), Ernst Thälmann, leader of the KPD, elaborated on this theory of 'social fascism'. According to his analysis the first great period of revolutionary awakening had ushered in the Bolshevik revolution in Russia, but this had been followed by a temporary stabilisation and consolidation of capitalism in western Europe. Now, Thälmann announced to the assembled delegates, this temporary period of stabilisation was at an end, and the class struggle would once again intensify. 'Therefore the greatest danger to the triumphant march of socialism' lay not so much in the disintegrating *bourgeoisie* and its representatives, but 'in the social democracy which gains the trust of the masses through fraud and treachery'. The task of social democracy, Thälmann proclaimed, was to frustrate the socialist transformation of society during a period of revolutionary upheaval (Protocols of the Fourth Congress of the Communist International).

The onset of the Great Depression apparently confirmed much of Thälmann's hypothesis. The steady rise in the KPD's membership and voting figures was surely proof of the radicalisation taking place among the German workers, as mass unemployment negated traditional trade-union-led responses to falling living standards. In 1928 the SPD obtained

111

During the Weimar Republic there was a flowering of proletarian culture which embraced not only the intellectual theatre of Brecht and Toller, and the artistic genius of Grosz, but also grass-roots organisations which developed and explored the traditions of German working-class life. *Above* Socialist Youth perform the folk-dance 'Sun-rose'. Agit-prop groups would often travel through the countryside performing at festivals and preaching their political message. *Below* An SPD theatre group in Nuremberg perform in a factory canteen.

nearly three votes for every one to the KPD. By November 1932, however, the ratio had closed to 12:10. The KPD therefore attracted those workers who were most affected by the steady decline of living standards under Brüning's government and who were appalled at the seeming impotence of the Social Democratic leadership in the face of the growing fascist menace. Yet, when Brüning's government finally fell, the leadership of the KPD declared, 'There is no difference in principle between a fascist dictatorship and a bourgeois dictatorship.' Indeed for Thälmann a Nazi dictatorship was an 'inevitable development' and certainly preferable to the rule of social democracy, for the working class would wage a united struggle against the naked aggression of National Socialism, while it was divided against itself in resisting the 'onslaught' of the SPD.

After 1928 the membership of the KPD underwent a dramatic change, largely as a result of the recession, but also because of

'Smash the world-foe!' Vote National Socialist.

A Nazi poster from 1928 showing an archetypal Nazi worker
smashing the Stock Exchange of 'international high-finance'.

'Socialism opens the factories.' Vote Communist List 4.

'Clear the way for List 1.' Social Democrats.

An SPD poster from 1930 identifying the Nazis and Communists
as equal enemies.

'Against civil war and inflation!!'

A German Nationalist poster (DNVP) produced for the Reichstag
elections of July 1932.

Ernst Thälmann (left) takes the salute at a march-past of KPD para-military units in Berlin 1929. Thälmann gained his early political experience in Hamburg where he was a transport worker. As leader he had immense courage and energy, but lacked real vision. His speeches were notable for his mixing of metaphors – 'like a new-born baby that has lost its way in the sand' – but what he lacked in finesse he made up for in his forceful delivery.

'*Right* 'Red Hamburg' on election day in 1931.

the policies which the KPD tenaciously followed. Whereas in 1928 63 per cent of party members were industrial workers, in 1932 industrial workers made up only 11 per cent of the party membership, and no less than 85 per cent of the party's membership was unemployed. This tendency was reflected in voting patterns as well. Those still in employment in 1932 remained largely loyal to the SPD and the Free Trade Unions, while those out of work registered their protest by voting Communist. Thus the KPD became not so much the party of the revolutionary workers as the political representative of the uprooted and dispossessed. The majority of Communist Party members lacked contact with the traditions of working-class organisation, and certainly they lacked the discipline necessary to

Above and below A mass meeting of the KPD 'Red Front' in Berlin.

wage a protracted political struggle. Few of the KPD leaders were older than forty while many rank-and-file activists were hardly out of their teens and unlikely to have been employed since entering the labour market. Even more alarming was the fact that most of the party activists had been members of the KPD for less than three years. The turnover of members was astonishing.

	entered	left	total 31 Dec
1929	50,000	39,000	130,000
1930	143,000	95,000	180,000
1931	210,000	130,000	260,000

(A. Aviv, *The SPD and KPD at the end of the Weimar Republic*).

In 1932 the turnover of members was 54 per cent, of whom a significant number left to join the NSDAP!

Unity and conflict

The way in which both working-class parties reacted to the von Papen coup in Prussia on 20 July 1932 exemplified the structural weakness of the German labour movement and foreshadowed its impotence in the face of the Nazis' openly terroristic attacks twelve months later. The SPD and the trade-union leadership were unwilling to call a General Strike because they feared the inevitable political confrontation that this would provoke, believing that in a situation of open conflict the workers would move to the left and that the KPD would gain influence at their expense. In the end the Social Democrats filed a pathetic legal complaint against von Papen which only underlined their unwillingness to oppose force with counter-force. The lesson of the Prussian *coup d'état* was not lost on Hitler, for the failure to act against the conservatives meant that the SPD's threat of mass action in the event of a Nazi take-over of power was quite hollow. The KPD on the other hand declared an immediate General Strike against von Papen, which, given the Communists' lack of influence within the factories, could not hope to be effective. Moreover the KPD's frequently stated indifference to the principles of parliamentary democracy made a nonsense of such support for constitutional legality, and it was no surprise when Thälmann later consoled the party for the failure with the news that von Papen's move would

The army in Wilhelmstraße in the government quarter of Berlin during von Papen's coup against the Prussian government, 20 July 1932.

After the spectacular success of the NSDAP in the Reichstag elections of 1930, the Social Democratic Party set up a number of specifically anti-fascist organisations to counter the threat of Nazism. *Above* The *Reichsbanner Schutzformationen* (Reichsbanner Defence Force) was founded in 1930 with approximately 160,000 members. The Magdeburg section gives the clenched fist salute. *Below* SPD Minister Severing addresses a meeting of the Reichsbanner at Koblenz in 1932.

4. The Last Act

Anti-fascist demonstration, 22 February 1931.

increase support for the Communists among the workers of Prussia.

In fact the German Communist Party, for all its revolutionary posturing and its statement in December 1932 that the time was ripe for 'revolution, the dictatorship of the proletariat and the establishment of a soviet Germany' (Comintern declaration, 'The KPD on the Offensive') was as much a revolutionary party in 1932 as the SPD had been in 1918. Indeed the parallels are ironic. Just as the Social Democratic leadership believed that socialism would come about in the twentieth century as a result of the 'laws of historical development', so the KPD believed that the crisis of world capitalism in the 1930s would 'inevitably' lead to the institution of a Communist state – even if a fascist dictatorship was a 'temporary inter-mediate development'. Similarly the SPD leadership in 1918 had 'held the masses on the halter' because they feared that allowing the working class to create its own democratic institutions based upon the work-place would inevitably unleash 'Bolshevism'. The Communist Party leadership in 1932, though it may have believed that a revolutionary struggle was necessary, also feared the blossoming of a radical democratic mass movement among the German working class. Long before the ignominious disintegration of the KPD, its leadership corps had been purged of any independent elements capable of challenging the party line as laid down by the Comintern. Thus, far from representing the interests of the German workers, by the late 1920s the KPD's political line was dancing to the tune of Stalin's foreign policy objectives.

Yet there is ample evidence that among the workers themselves, both Socialists and Communists were prepared to sink their wider political differences and join together to fight fascism. The political leaders of both parties were thus forced to the extreme of warning members not to co-operate with working-class 'opponents' in the day-to-day struggle against the menace of Nazism. The offensives of the SPD and the KPD were too often directed not at the

117

Shortly before the November elections (1932) a major transport strike erupted in Berlin as a result of von Papen's attempt to cut wages. The SPD and the Free Trade Unions declined to support the workers. The Communist Party and the Nazis made common cause to back the strike. *Above* A member of the Nazi 'Factory Organization' (NSBO) (left) and a Communist member of the 'Revolutionary Trade Unions' form a picket during the Transport Strike. *Below* Sabotaged tramlines in Berlin during the strike.

common enemy but at each other. The consolidation of their respective party organisations among the working class and the unemployed became an end in itself, and not a means towards the transformation of German society into a Socialist republic – whether based upon parliamentary democracy or revolutionary soviets.

Under the dictatorship of the Kaiser the German labour movement had been distinguished by great political theorists such as Karl Kautsky, Karl Liebknecht and, above all, Rosa Luxemburg. The tragedy of the November Revolution was that the German working class lacked a mature political organisation capable and *willing* to lead revolutionary sentiment into productive channels, so that democratic institutions based upon the particular cultural traditions of the German working class might flourish. In retrospect the German Communist Party was still-born at birth. The refusal of the majority of delegates to accept Rosa Luxemburg's criticisms of the Bolshevik 'model' of revolution and her plea for a long-term strategy based upon 'educating the masses' closed the one avenue of development that could have allowed the German working

e Front von vorn

Die Front von hinten

An SPD leaflet identifies the Nazis and the Communists as one and the same enemy. 'The Front marching forward' displays the Nazi swastika. 'Down with Marxism' is the slogan 'The Front from the rear' displays the Communist Red Star. 'Down with the SPD' is the slogan.

On the day his books were burned by the Nazis, Ernst Toller wrote to the German workers:

We must not seek excuses for our faults, our failures or our crimes.
If we are to be honest, we must have knowledge.
If we are to be brave, we must understand.
If we want justice, we must never forget.

On 22 May 1939, after six years in exile, Toller committed suicide.

The Leadership of the Iron Front (Berlin) gives the following answer:

... the organisations united in the Iron Front are absolutely convinced that a *unification of the proletariat is more essential than ever before.* The fascist danger demands this unity. The danger of fascism however can only be countered when a *genuine* common will to unity is present. At the demonstration of the Iron Front on June 9th, comrades Künstler and Aufhäser referred to the possibility of all proletarian organisations joining together to fight fascism. As a precondition for this we demanded that the *attacks of the communist party against our organisations and leaders should stop.* You refer in your letter of June 16th to the call published in the Red Flag on the same day. This proclamation includes, in contrast to your offer of forming a united front, a whole series of unjust and damaging attacks upon our organisations, our functionaries and our leadership. Attacks which hardly point to an honest desire to join a common struggle against fascism.

We agree with you that the ban on demonstrations must be lifted. We have already taken our petition to the relevant authorities. But you have made it impossible to pursue the necessary united front against fascism because of your year-long attempts to subvert and dismember strong workers' organisations, your common cause with the fascists both inside and outside parliament, your attempts to cripple the Trade Union movement through the Revolutionary Trade Unions, and your slogans, 'Severing – the same as Hitler' and 'Social Democracy – the real enemy'.

When you have honestly met the necessary preconditions as set out above, the Iron Front sees no reason why a united front should not be forged.

Reply of the Iron Front (SPD anti-fascist Front) to the KPD's proposals, in *Vorwärts,* 18 June 1932.

The Berlin Area Communist Party demands:

Make Way for the Anti-Fascist Demonstration!

To the area leadership of the German Trade Union Federation, the Social Democratic Party and the Reichsbanner.

The area leadership of Berlin Brandenburg KPD has sent the following call for a united mass demonstration in Berlin, under the slogan 'Mass Demonstration! Political Strike!'

Because a unified demonstration of the working masses in Berlin would be a blow against fascism and a means of strengthening the fighting spirit of the proletariat, we have suggested in our proclamation of 16 June that a unified demonstration be called of all workers and their organisations. Our battle cry must be:

Down with fascist reactionaries!

Away with the von Papen government!

Down with imperialist war. Defend the Soviet Union!

This suggestion is in line with *the will of the working masses* as expressed by the workers in numerous resolutions in the factories, in offices and in working class quarters.

In the meantime we have discovered that the Prussian government is formally maintaining the ban on demonstrations. This measure serves only the cause of fascism, since the mobilisation of the workers against fascist terror is thereby weakened. Therefore in the interests of strengthening the mass struggle against fascism we ask you to support the demands of the overwhelming mass of workers in calling for an immediate reinstatement of the freedom to demonstrate for all organisations which are ready to fight against fascism. Indeed we recall that in similar circumstances before the war the Social Democratic Party brought the workers out onto the streets in reply to a ban on demonstrations.

... we await your reply until the 18th of June.

with proletarian greetings,

KPD Berlin Brandenburg.   W. Ulbricht.   16 June 1932.

Article in the KPD *Red Flag* demanding anti-fascist unity, 17 June 1932.

class to go forward and build upon the modest gains of November 1918.

In 1932, when six million workers were sufficiently desperate to throw their weight behind a German Communist Party, despite its obvious flaws and weaknesses, and when those workers loyal to the Social Democrats expected the republican *Reichsbanner* to offer genuine resistence to the Nazi onslaught, the leadership of the German labour movement can only be characterised as 'colourless, mediocre and lacking in imagination and initiative' (A. Aviv). While the SPD was paralysed by fear of using extra-parliamentary action to defend democracy and the republic, the KPD appeared blind or indifferent to the concrete realities of German society and relied upon a foreign party apparatus for guidance and the formulation of political policies. Thus in the hour of decision – a decision of life or death for many thousands of German workers – the rank and file were unable to exert their will upon the two parties which claimed to be their political representatives. Both the SPD and the KPD were *undemocratic* in the real sense of the word. Each was a functionary corps whose inertia left it unable and unwilling to react to changes in political circumstances. Indeed it is not too gross an oversimplification to suggest that both Communist and Social Democratic party functionaries were prepared to see the annihilation of the entire German labour movement rather than accept that the struggle for its very survival might necessitate the weakening of their respective party organisations.

The take-over of power

On the day he was appointed Chancellor, Hitler presided over the first meeting of the Nationalist cabinet. In line with the brief given by Hindenburg, the cabinet was formally committed to securing majority support in the Reichstag, and Goering duly reported on the possibility of gaining the support of the Catholic Centre Party. If agreement could not be reached, Hitler announced, there would be no alternative to the holding of new elections. Hugenberg balked at this suggestion, but he was equally hostile to the participation of the Centre Party in a coalition government. Within a matter of days he was out-manoeuvered as Hitler saw to it that the coalition talks failed, and Hindenberg was persuaded to sign a decree dissolving the Reichstag. This time the German electorate was to go to the polls with the resources of the state behind the NSDAP. 'Radio and Press are at our disposal,' Goebbels wrote in his diary on 3 February; 'even money is not lacking'.

Indeed money was not lacking. On 22 February Germany's leading industrialists were summoned to Goering's palace to be told that the election would be the last for the next decade, if not for a hundred years. Should the election fail to prove decisive, Hitler added, other means would be used. Goering closed the meeting with the following appeal: 'Those circles not taking part in the political battle should at least make the financial sacrifices necessary at this time' (Nuremberg Document D203). Those present donated the sum of three million Reichsmarks for the election campaign fund.

Official figures alone show that fifty-one persons were killed and hundreds badly injured during the election campaign. Nazi Stormtroopers broke up the meetings of non-Nationalist parties. Left-wing candidates were threatened, abused, beaten up and, in a number of cases, murdered. Newspapers which spoke out against Hitler and Nazi brutality were suppressed. In Prussia Goering announced that it was the duty of the police to aid all forms of Nationalist propaganda, but to show no mercy against those organisations 'hostile to the state'. On 22 February Goering created a 50,000-strong auxiliary police unit to augment the regular force: 25,000 of its men were drawn from the SA and 15,000 from the SS. Two days later the 'police' staged a raid on the KPD's headquarters in Berlin where they 'discovered' plans outlining a Communist plot to topple the government. Publication of the details, though promised, never materialised, but circumstantial evidence was mysteriously provided on the night of 27 February, when the Reichstag building went up in flames. A Dutch Communist by the name of van der Lubbe was arrested in the grounds of the building and subsequently

Above Hitler meets leading industrialists and businessmen shortly after the take-over of power.

Below Arrested 'leftists' held captive by SA 'auxiliaries'.

Social Democratic political prisoners arrive at
Oranienburg Concentration Camp, August 1933.

charged with arson. This act, claimed
Goering, was the signal for a Marxist
uprising. The mass arrest of leading Communists followed swiftly, though the
Reichstag Fire trial later ended in fiasco
when all but van der Lubbe were acquitted
of involvement. Nevertheless in the atmosphere of anti-Communist hysteria whipped
up by the authorities and the media it was
possible for measures suspending constitutional liberties and authorising the Reich
government to take control in the federal
states to be pushed through. Where these
powers proved insufficient for the Nazis'
purposes, Goering boasted in Frankfurt on
3 March: 'Our measures will not be
crippled by judicial niceties ... My mission
is to destroy and exterminate – nothing
more, nothing less. So, dear Communists,
don't get the wrong idea. I shall lead a
struggle to the death at the head of the
Brownshirts, in which I will grab you by

the throat with my fist.' (Nuremberg
Document 1856-PS).

Yet despite the atmosphere of terror and
intimidation which accompanied the
election campaign, the Nazis only just
achieved an overall majority in the
Reichstag with the aid of their Nationalist
partners. On the other hand, with the pro-
scription of the KPD (the Communists had
achieved nearly 5 million votes in the elections and returned 81 deputies) the
NSDAP alone could claim a parliamentary majority. Absolute power was
within Hitler's grasp.

On 24 March, when the Reichstag
assembled in the Kroll Opera House to
debate the Enabling Bill, Hitler made the
opening speech. The Bill provided for the
Chancellor to draft and enact legislation
without parliamentary approval. Most
Communist deputies were already in
prison, and those Social Democrats still at
liberty had to brave the intimidation of
massed ranks of SS and SA men who ringed

The SA occupy the offices of the German Trade
Unions in Munich on 2 May 1933

the Opera House and thronged the
corridors inside. The Nazis needed a two-
thirds majority to carry their Bill, and in
the circumstances it was a mere formality.
At the last moment even the Catholic
Centre Party gave its assent, so drawing to
a close its inglorious career as a democratic party under Weimar and opening a
new chapter of sordid compromise under
the Third Reich. When the votes had been
counted, Goering declared that 441
deputies had voted in favour – 94 against.
The Nazis, already masters of the streets,
were now masters of the state.

On 1 April the SA imposed a boycott of Jewish
shops.

On 7 April a law was promulgated to remove
'non-Aryans' and 'politically unreliable' civil
servants from their posts.

On 26 April the *Geheimen Staats Polizeiamt*
or *Gestapo* was formed in Berlin.

On 2 May Trade Union offices were ransacked
by the SA. Trade Unions were declared illegal.

On 22 June the German Social Democratic
Party was banned.

Between 27 June and 5 July all political parties
except the NSDAP were 'dissolved'.

On 20 March the first concentration camp for
political prisoners was opened in an old munitions
factory in Dachau near Munich.
Three weeks later three inmates were shot dead
'attempting to escape'.

By the end of 1933, over 150,000 political
prisoners had been incarcerated in over one
hundred concentration camps throughout
Germany.

The books of 'un-German' authors are burned
outside Berlin University.

On 10 May the books of 'un-German'
authors were burned in public bonfires
throughout Germany, including works by
Sigmund Freud, Albert Einstein, Bertolt
Brecht, Heinrich Mann, Karl Marx, and
Ernst Toller.

That was only a prelude.
Those who burn books
Will in the end
Burn men!
    (Heinrich Heine, 1820)

Bibliographical Notes

Much of the material in this book is based upon documentary sources, in particular from the *Bayerisches Hauptstaatsarchiv* and the *Institut für Zeitgeschichte* in Munich. Equally a great deal of secondary material has been drawn from German texts not available in English translation.

For the English reader the following is a very brief guide to works that can be recommended for more detailed reading:

Still one of the best overall studies of the German labour movement, despite the early date of its publication is Evelyn Anderson, *Hammer or Anvil, The Story of the German Working Class Movement* (London 1945), which should be read in conjunction with Carl Schorske's quite excellent book, *German Social Democracy: the Development of the Great Schism* (Cambridge Mass. 1955) for an understanding of the early history of German Social Democracy. Charles Burdick and Ralph Lutz deal with the November Revolution in *The Political Institutions of the German Revolution* (New York 1966), although a really thorough work on the subject in English awaits its historian. Allan Mitchell's *Revolution in Bavaria 1918-1919* (Princeton 1965) is a good introduction to the history of the Bavarian Workers Republic, while Rosa Leviné-Meyer's biography of her husband Eugen Leviné provides an interesting (if wholly personal) insight into a complex period. W.T. Angress, *Stillborn Revolution* (New York 1963), remains the major English work on the early history of the German Communist Party, but David

Morgan, *The Socialist Left and the German Revolution* (Cornell University 1975), has added a lot of new material on the Independent Socialists and this is a first-class addition to our knowledge of the early years of Weimar.

The mechanics and the political effects of hyper-inflation are covered by F. Ringer (ed.), *The German Inflation of 1923* (London 1969). F.L. Carsten covers the role of the army under Weimar in *Reichswehr and Politics 1918-1933* (Oxford 1966).

The ideological origins of National Socialism are examined by George Mosse, *The Crisis of German Ideology* (London 1966) and by Fritz Stern, *The Politics of Cultural Despair* (New York 1961). A history of the Freecorps movement is provided by Robert Waite, *The Vanguard of Nazism* (Cambridge Mass. 1952).

Nazism has been the excuse for a seemingly endless wave of sensational and nonsensical books about Adolf Hitler, including those that now attempt to deny Hitler's role in the extermination of the Jews. In contrast is Alan Bullock's weighty biography *Hitler: a study in tyranny* (London 1952) – a carefully researched book which places Hitler within an historical context. Sound general works on the rise of German fascism include Karl D. Bracher, *The German Dictatorship* (London 1970) and Dietrich Orlow, *A History of the Nazi Party 1919-1933* (Pittsburgh 1969). More detailed works of interest are Jeremy Noakes, *The Nazi Party in Lower Saxony 1921-1933* (Oxford 1971); Geoffrey Pridham, *Hitler's Rise to Power and the Nazi Movement in Bavaria*

1923-1933 (London 1973); and Peter Merkl, *Political Violence under the Swastika* (Princeton 1975) which uses data from Abel's study of Nazi party members and provides an essential insight into why 'ordinary Germans' supported Hitler.

Sadly lacking in English is an up-to-date examination of the links between the NSDAP and its supporters, both among the *Mittelstand* and in the business community. The way in which the business community and the conservative establishment helped Hitler to power is detailed in documents presented at the Nuremberg Trials and published as *The Trial of the Major War Criminals before the International Military Tribunal Proceedings*, vols 1-23, and *Documents in Evidence*, vols 24-42 – not only are the contents of these documents often forgotten, they also provide uncomfortable reading for those enjoying status and privilege in West Germany today.

Index